KENT NATURE WALKS

Michael Easterbrook

COUNTRYSIDE BOOKS

NEWBURY, BERKSHIRE

COUNTRYSIDE BOOKS
3 Catherine Road
Newbury, Berkshire

To view our complete range of books,
please visit us at
www.countrysidebooks.co.uk

ISBN 1 85306 787 3

*Dedicated to the staff and volunteers
of Kent Wildlife Trust and Butterfly Conservation*

Designed by Graham Whiteman
Maps by the author
Photographs by the author and Vernon Hucks

Produced through MRM Associates Ltd., Reading
Typeset by Techniset Typesetters, Newton-le-Willows
Printed in Italy

Contents

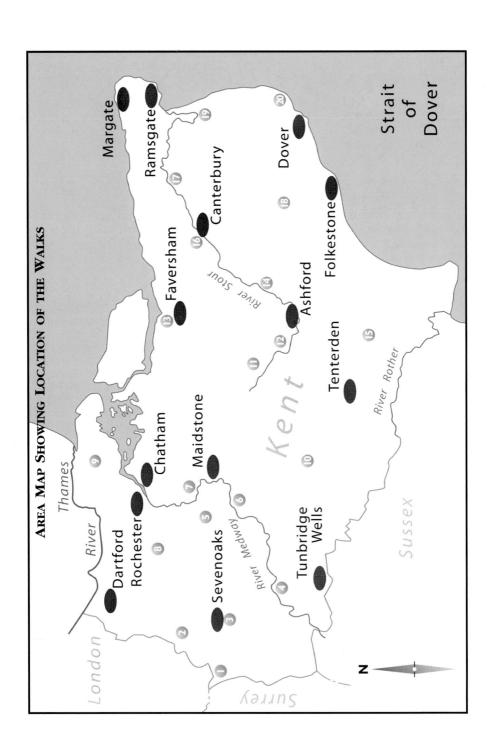

AREA MAP SHOWING LOCATION OF THE WALKS

Walk

PUBLISHER'S NOTE

We hope that you obtain considerable enjoyment from this book; great care has been taken in its preparation. Although at the time of publication all routes followed public rights of way or permitted paths, diversion orders can be made and permissions withdrawn.

We cannot, of course, be held responsible for such diversion orders and any inaccuracies in the text which result from these or any other changes to the routes nor any damage which might result from walkers trespassing on private property. We are anxious though that all details covering the walks are kept up to date and would therefore welcome information from readers which would be relevant to future editions.

The simple sketch maps that accompany the walks in this book are based on notes made by the author whilst checking out the routes on the ground. However, for the benefit of a proper map, we do recommend that you purchase the relevant Ordnance Survey sheet covering your walk. The Ordnance Survey maps are widely available, especially through booksellers and local newsagents.

INTRODUCTION

Despite its position as the gateway to the Continent, Kent still has some lovely countryside and a fine variety of habitats for wildlife. Its proximity to continental Europe and relatively hot, dry climate means that some flowers and animals are able to survive here on the northern edge of their range, but not in other parts of Britain. One of the richest habitats is the grassland of the North Downs, where the short turf may contain as many as 40 different wild flowers in one square metre, and 28 types of butterfly may be seen. Many beautiful wild orchids can also be found here and there are wonderful scents from wild herbs, such as thyme and marjoram.

Kent also has a long coastline, so consequently has a good variety of birds and other wildlife that feed and nest on sand or shingle beaches or on the coastal marshes. There are river estuaries whose mudflats attract teeming hordes of ducks, geese and waders and several rivers, including the Medway, Darent and Stour, flow through Kent and provide habitats for freshwater wildlife. Where gravel has been extracted the flooded pits also provide feeding areas for water birds. Elsewhere, on the heavy clay soils of the Weald, there are many streams and ponds, while Romney Marsh is criss-crossed with drainage ditches, a sanctuary for colourful dragonflies and aquatic plants. Kent also has remnants of ancient woodland, vibrant with colour in spring as bluebells, wood anemones and celandines rush into flower before the trees come into leaf and cast shade.

The contrasts between the different types of countryside, from the hills of the North Downs, Greensand Ridge and High Weald to the river valleys, coastal strip and flatlands of the North Kent and Romney Marshes, provide interesting walks with fine views. This enjoyment is enhanced by typical Kentish scenes of fruit orchards and oasthouses, preserving its reputation as 'the Garden of England'. The walks in this book will take you through examples of these varied types of countryside and I have indicated a selection of the flora and fauna to look out for on the way. The walks involving woodland are at their best in the spring, when wild flowers are in bloom, or in autumn when the leaves turn to red and gold. In June and July the downland walks are at their most colourful with flowers and butterflies. Coastal walks are good at any time of year, though the populations of birds on the marshes and mudflats are often at their highest in the winter months. There are nature notes for each walk to provide more information on some of the flowers or animals that you may see. Please do not disturb the wildlife, and leave the flowers for others to enjoy.

Because much of Kent's countryside is undulating, many of the walks involve some climbs and descents, though these are usually gradual. Paths can often be muddy, so suitable footwear is recommended. Road walking has been kept to a minimum but short stretches are sometimes included so take care, particularly if walking with children. Sketch maps of the walks are provided, but I recommend that you also have the appropriate Ordnance Survey Explorer map that covers that area. Binoculars and wildlife field guides can also be useful.

Several of the walks visit nature reserves. If you want to find out more about these contact Kent Wildlife Trust (01622 662012), RSPB (01273 775333) or English Nature (01233 812525). Kent Wildlife Trust and the RSPB have programmes of guided walks and also wildlife activities for children.

Directions for travel by car and places to park are provided for each walk. However, it is more environmentally friendly to travel by public transport, and most of the walks are accessible by bus or train. For up-to-date timetables contact Traveline (0870 6082608, www.traveline.org.uk) or National Rail Enquiries (08457 484950, www.totaljourney.com). Kent County Council produces an excellent public transport map and there is also information on their website: www.kentpublictransport.info.

The 20 walks in this book are all circular and range in length from $2^3/_4$ to $7^1/_2$ miles (most less than 6). Information is provided on a nearby pub where refreshment can be obtained, and in some cases a tearoom is available too. There are also details of places to visit close to the walk, if you want to include them in your day out. I hope you enjoy these walks through Kent's lovely countryside and see plenty of interesting wildlife.

Michael Easterbrook

WESTERHAM, MARINERS HILL AND FRENCH STREET

– *bluebell woods and views to hills*

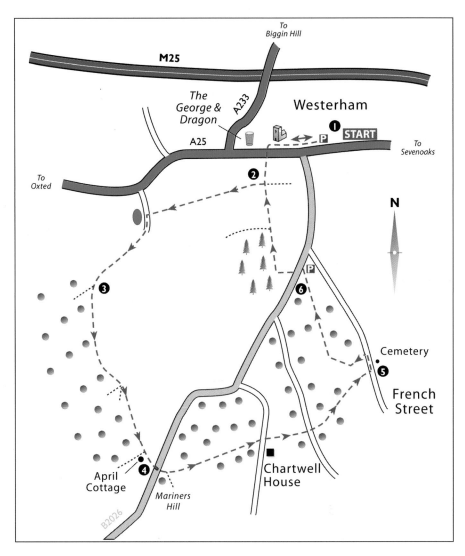

*S*tarting at Westerham, a village with historical associations with Winston Churchill and General Wolfe, this walk takes you through the lovely wooded countryside to the south. The woods are full of bluebells and other flowers in spring, and in autumn the leaves display wonderful colours of gold, bronze and red. You will also see lots of toadstools in the woods in autumn and may even glimpse a deer. As a bonus there are some glorious views across to the North Downs as you return to Westerham.

THE WALK

1 From the public car park take the path past an information board, between houses, and through the churchyard to the village green. Bear left past the statue of Winston Churchill, cross the main road, and go up steps to a narrow passageway called Water Lane, by a Greensand Way signpost. Go down this passageway between gardens, crossing two streams, to a kissing gate.

2 Turn sharp right after the gate to walk parallel with the stream. In the meadow you may see butterflies such as the pretty small

STARTING POINT: At the public car park alongside the A25 to the east of the village.

HOW TO GET THERE: Westerham is on the A25 between Oxted and Sevenoaks, at the junction with the A233. Go to the eastern edge of the village on the A25 to find the car park on the north side of the road. Metrobus and Southlands Travel buses serve Westerham.

PARKING: In the large free car park at the eastern fringe of Westerham.

REFRESHMENTS: The car park is a short distance from the village green and main street where there are several pubs and three tearooms. The George & Dragon is in the centre of the village and serves a good selection of meals and snacks. Telephone: 01959 563071.

LENGTH OF WALK: 5 miles. Map: OS Explorer 147 Sevenoaks & Tonbridge (GR 450542).

copper and the orange and brown gatekeeper. Go past large ash, horse chestnut and alder trees to the end of the meadow, where you cross a footbridge to a lane. Opposite is a large pond where dragonflies skim over the surface and coot skulk in the reedmace. Turn left on the road and to the left of a lodge house, then immediately sharp right on a path, not straight on. The path goes gradually uphill, with fine views back over Westerham to the North Downs. As the path bends left there is a Turkey oak on the right, with its curious 'hairy' acorn cups. The broad grassy track continues between fences to a stile, then crosses a meadow to another. After this go diagonally right through a clump of beech, oak and sweet chestnut trees to a stile in front of a farm track, with woods beyond.

3 Turn left on the track alongside the wood, full of bluebells in spring and with a good mixture of trees, including oak and birch, with holly beneath. There are speckled wood, peacock and holly blue butterflies here and colourful flowers such as yellow gorse and purple rosebay willowherb. Continue to a stile next to a metal gate and straight on to another stile, with masses of bluebells under the trees on the right. Now go slightly away from the wood, to cross a meadow to a stile near a converted oasthouse. After the stile go sharp left on a path alongside a wooden garden fence. You pass some huge ash and beech trees, with yew and holly beneath, and you may be lucky enough to spot a deer here. At a

The familiar peacock butterfly has the characteristic brightly-coloured 'eye-spots' on its wings, reminiscent of those on the tail of the bird. When alarmed by a potential predator such as a bird it can suddenly open its wings with an audible click and flash these eye-spots to scare it. The spiky, shiny black caterpillars of the peacock feed in large groups on nettles, while the adult butterflies can often be seen feeding on the nectar of flowers such as thistles, knapweeds, buddleia and teasel. Here it is on bluebells, which carpet many woods in Kent in the spring, particularly on the heavier soils.

The small copper is a tiny but lovely butterfly, with wings of a burnished copper colour and reddish and blue markings. The caterpillars feed on docks and sorrels. The butterfly is rarely seen in large numbers but individuals may be found in a variety of habitats, visiting flowers or basking in the sun on a patch of bare ground.

marker post near tall pine trees keep straight on, but soon go diagonally left at the next marker post, past the drive to April Cottage and continue to a road.

4 Cross with care to a path at a bridleway sign at Mariners Hill and go uphill past gnarled beech trunks and holly bushes, the path strewn with beech mast in autumn. At the top of the slope turn left at a post with a Greensand Way (GW) marker, to go through a wood with birch trees festooned with wild honeysuckle and with lots of rhododendrons. Go straight across any cross-tracks, following the GW markers, then downhill and down steps to a road opposite the entrance to Chartwell House. Go straight across to a footpath that goes uphill between hedges, with foxgloves among the trees. On reaching a minor road go straight across to a bridleway, a wide sandy track through birch trees, with bilberry beneath. Keep right where the path forks, to go between tall hedges with houses behind, and reach a road.

5 This is French Street – go left up the road, ignoring footpaths going off right, and past a private cemetery with a 400 year old yew tree. After another 50 yards turn left up a narrow tarmac lane opposite house number 3. After 300 yards, as the lane bends downhill, go right at a marker post opposite the house sign for Brackenwood. Follow the path through yews and pines, directed by yellow arrows on marker posts, and keeping straight on at any cross-paths. There are lots of toadstools to see in autumn, and the path eventually emerges in a small, stony car park.

6 Keep to the left edge of the car park to a road, then go left for 50 yards and cross to a footpath sign. The path goes to the left of a beech hedge in front of stables, then through trees with heather, bilberry and rhododendron beneath. After a short section of plank walkway reach a T-junction with a cross-track at a marker post. Turn right here, to continue with tall conifers on the left. After more plank walkway go between posts then bear right past more conifers. Keep diagonally right at a tall marker post, then as the broad track swings left go down to the right on a parallel track to a stile. Turn right past oak and beech trees on the edge of a meadow then diagonally left to a stile, with glorious views ahead to the Downs. Continue downhill to the kissing gate at Point 2 and straight along the passageway back to the village green.

PLACES OF INTEREST NEARBY

Chartwell (National Trust) was the family home of Sir Winston Churchill for over 40 years and has mementoes of his life and a lovely garden. Two miles south of Westerham. Telephone: 01732 866368. **Squerryes Court** is a beautiful 17th century manor house with fine furniture and paintings set in a landscaped garden with lake. Signposted from the A25, 1/2 mile west of Westerham. Telephone: 01959 562345.

SHOREHAM, THE DARENT VALLEY AND LULLINGSTONE PARK

– *riverbank, ancient woods and flower-filled meadows*

*T*he chance to explore a variety of habitats in the beautiful Darent Valley, the inspiration for paintings by Samuel Palmer. The walk takes you alongside the river, with the possibility of seeing herons, kingfishers and grey wagtails. Later you walk through Lullingstone Park, once a deer park, where there are ancient woods, rich in birds, insects and toadstools, and very old pollarded trees with massive gnarled trunks. There is also chalk downland full of colourful wild flowers and butterflies, and there are lovely views. The walk includes gradual climbs and descents.

STARTING POINT: At the public car park, on the south-west side of Shoreham village.

HOW TO GET THERE: Shoreham is 4 miles north of Sevenoaks, just off the A225. Going north on the A225 turn left near Shoreham station and go through the village to a T-junction, then left to the car park. Shoreham railway station, 1/2 mile from the

village, is on the London Blackfriars to Sevenoaks line, and Arriva buses run an infrequent service to the village.

PARKING: In the public car park in Filston Road in Shoreham.

REFRESHMENTS: There are three pubs in the village. The King's Arms is open all day, with a wide selection of beers and food. It is probably the only pub that still has an ostler's box, where the ostler would look after the horses of the customers, though it is now occupied only by a lifelike model. Telephone: 01959 523100. Lullingstone Park visitor centre, passed on the walk, has a good café.

LENGTH OF WALK: 5³/₄ miles. Map: OS Explorer 147 Sevenoaks & Tonbridge (GR 518615).

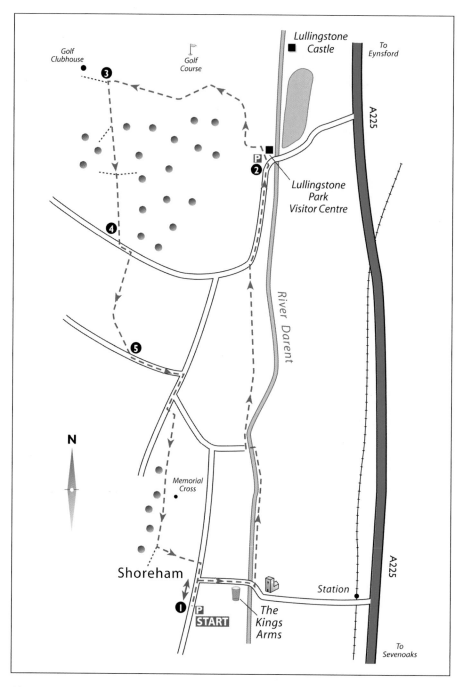

THE WALK

1 Going out of the entrance to the public car park turn right for 100 yards then right again down Church Street. Pass the King's Arms after 200 yards and shortly afterwards cross a bridge over the river, where there are often grey and pied wagtails near the water. Turn immediately left into Darent Way and walk alongside the River Darent, lined by willow and lime trees and later by tall alders and horse chestnuts. Follow the tarmac path and just past a row of cottages on the opposite bank turn left over a footbridge to reach a minor road. Turn immediately right onto a footpath by an information board, soon with the river on the right, where you may see a heron fishing. Continue through a kissing gate and along the right edge of a field to a stile, then diagonally left across the next field to another stile. You may see swifts swooping overhead as they hunt for insects. Cross a farm road and go straight on to another stile, then on a path between fields, with views to the North Downs on the right. Just past a small hop garden on the right reach a road and continue along it in the same direction, passing the farm shop at Castle Farm, then further on, where the road bends right, turn left into the Lullingstone Park visitor centre.

2 Unless pausing for refreshments, continue to the left of the centre's buildings to the far end of the car park and go through a kissing gate on the left, then gradually uphill on a wide mown path, passing picnic benches on the left. The tall hedge on the right has a good mixture of species, including hazel, wild cherry, field maple and hawthorn and various native trees have been planted on the left. Where the hedge on the right ends turn right at a post by a seat onto a track. Keep straight on where another hedge on the right ends after 100 yards. On the left is a meadow, colourful with buttercups, red clover and ox-eye daisies. Follow a series of posts with blue rings to a golf course and keep to the right of the golf

Trees, such as this oak, were often pollarded to protect them from the ravages of deer. Pollarding involved trimming the branches at a height of 6 to 15 ft to prevent the deer from eating the shoots. Such trees in Lullingstone Park are several hundred years old and provide homes for rare insects and lichens.

The attractive speckled wood butterfly can be seen during much of the year from April to October, as it has three generations. It frequents the edges of woods, woodland clearings and hedgerows, where its coloration of creamy-yellow spots on a dark brown background provides excellent camouflage as it basks on a leaf in the dappled sunshine. The males have territories, and will chase away other butterflies.

green ahead to a post by two wooden seats. Go left here to a post between small clumps of silver birch trees, then follow a wide mown path marked at intervals by posts (these have a green arrow on the *opposite* side). The path goes past meadows full of flowers, with skylarks singing overhead. Just past a golf tee on the right take the left fork in the path. The grassland on the left has lots of typical chalk downland flowers, including man, pyramidal, spotted and fragrant orchids in June, while purple knapweeds attract butterflies such as common and chalkhill blues, meadow browns and gatekeepers. Continue downhill to a stony track and turn right to follow it through the golf course, going gradually uphill with posts with blue rings at intervals, and bladder campion and crosswort at the base of the hedge on the right. Continue straight ahead where a metalled track comes in from the right and, 200 yards on, pass a pollarded oak tree on the left with a massive trunk, hollow in the centre. Keep on the track, with fine views looking back, until 200 yards before the golf clubhouse ahead on the right.

3 Go left here at a wooden fingerpost with left arrow saying 'circular walk footpath no 206' to a grass path going to the right of a golf green to enter a wood by a post. Continue under tall beeches to a golf fairway and go straight across to a wide path between trees. After 50 yards go diagonally left on a narrower grass path past tall hornbeam, ash and horse chestnut trees. Further on notice the dead tree trunk on the left, 10 yards back from the path, now home to families of woodpeckers. There are speckled wood butterflies and a fine variety of toadstools in autumn. At a crossroads of paths with a wooden fingerpost sign go straight across to a gate in a metal fence. Next to the gate is a ladder stile, dating from when Lullingstone Park was a deer park. A narrow path leads to a stile, then continue along the right edge of a field and down steps with caution to a lane.

4 Go left for 150 yards then right along a farm track. Where the track ends keep right of a garage and new bungalow then between hedges and along the right edge of a field with a hedge of pink may blossom and climbing bryony on the right. Go past a small copse of trees on the right to a dilapidated stile and a fine view ahead, then diagonally left downhill along the left edge of a meadow with a diverse range of chalkland flowers, including blue germander speedwell and milkwort, yellow buttercups and bird's-foot trefoil and white ox-eye daisies.

5 On reaching a minor road go left along it between an avenue of tall beech trees. At a T-junction go right then soon take the right fork where the road divides. After 100 yards go left at a footpath sign, taking the upper, wider path of two, then after 30 yards turn right by a metal barrier to a wide track under trees. Where the track forks at Meenfield Wood keep left of the wood, with fine views over Shoreham and the Darent Valley on the left and more colourful flowers on the bank on the right. Continue past the memorial cross carved in the chalk on the left until reaching wide steps on the left, opposite a wooden seat. Go left down the steps and downhill to reach the village past a row of old lime trees. At the main village street turn right for 300 yards to return to the car park.

PLACES OF INTEREST NEARBY

Lullingstone Roman Villa (English Heritage) has fine mosaic floors and remains of several rooms including a bath house, all under cover. Telephone: 01322 863467. **Lullingstone Castle** is a Tudor manor house with an impressive 16th century gatehouse. Telephone: 01322 862114. Both places are 3 miles north of Shoreham and accessed from the A225 at Eynsford.

KNOLE PARK

– herds of deer and ancient trees

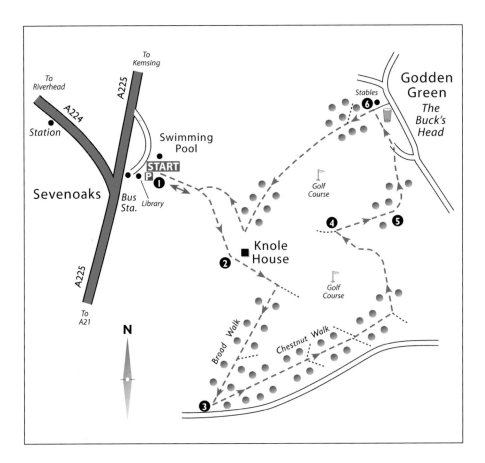

*T*his walk is mainly within the ancient and scenic parkland surrounding the magnificent Knole House, a huge medieval mansion. You will see herds of deer and impressive avenues of trees. There is a good diversity of bird life, and you are likely to see or hear a woodpecker. The walk also goes through woods made purple with rhododendrons in May and with red rowan berries in autumn, and there are lovely views to the Downs.

THE WALK

1 From the long stay car park in Sevenoaks (Buckhurst No 2) walk to its bottom end away from the town to the right hand corner, the opposite side to the swimming pool, and onto a tarmac path. Turn left to go downhill under overhanging branches and through a gate into Knole Park. Go straight across a valley where there are tall oaks, beeches and sweet chestnuts and herds of deer, and up to an estate road. Continue straight on over a hill, noticing the mistletoe growing on the trees on its crest. You soon see the impressive Knole House ahead. Aim for the far right corner of the walled garden to the right of the house.

2 At the corner of the wall, continue with it on your left, with ferns growing in cracks between the stones. Where the wall ends keep straight on to the right of a clump of conifers and observe the mosses and lichens growing on the ground here. On reaching a broad stony cross-track after 400 yards turn right on it, keeping straight on where

STARTING POINT: At the large public car park in Sevenoaks.

HOW TO GET THERE: From Sevenoaks High Street (A225) follow the signs to the swimming pool, library and long stay car park. Arriva and Metrobus buses go to Sevenoaks from various locations and the bus station is close to the start. Sevenoaks railway station is 1 mile from the start.

PARKING: In the long stay car park in Sevenoaks near the library and swimming pool, known as Buckhurst No 2 car park.

REFRESHMENTS: There are many pubs, restaurants and cafés in Sevenoaks and a tearoom at Knole House. The Buck's Head at Godden Green is a friendly country pub, requiring only a short diversion from the walk, or it is 2 miles from Sevenoaks by road. It has a separate eating area and pleasant garden and is open daily at lunchtime and in the evenings. Telephone: 01732 761330.

LENGTH OF WALK: 5½ miles. Map: OS Explorer 147 Sevenoaks & Tonbridge (GR 533547).

another track leaves it on the left after 100 yards. This track, known as the Broad Walk, is lined by tall oak trees, many of which suffered damage during the 1987 storm and now have spectacular fungi growing on the damaged branches. The short turf alongside the track is studded with the yellow flowers of tormentil in high summer and there are patches of purple rosebay willowherb in the woods.

3 After ³/₄ mile, go left on another broad track that goes diagonally back to the left, soon passing large tree stumps on the right. This avenue is lined by tall sweet chestnut trees and is called the Chestnut Walk. Notice the convoluted, furrowed patterns on the bark and the spiky cases of the nuts. You may see common blue butterflies at the side of the track, and on the ragwort plants with their yellow daisy-like flowers are the yellow and black hooped caterpillars of the cinnabar moth. The adult moths often fly during the day and are also colourful, being pinky-red and black. In places there are mountain ash (or rowan trees) in the woods with bunches of vivid red berries, popular with birds. Keep straight on where the Greensand Way footpath crosses the track (with a marker post on the right) after almost ³/₄ mile and continue to where the broad tarmac path ends, then keep on for 10 yards to a narrow tarmac road that crosses your path. Go left on this road and follow it past Keeper's Cottage on the left, then a pond that has large dragonflies swooping over it in summer. Cross a golf fairway with care, then the road goes down into a dip and up again, before bending left.

Fallow deer, having died out in Britain in the Ice Age, were probably reintroduced here by the Normans, and they were then conserved in deer parks by kings and noblemen. Their spotted coat provides good camouflage when they are in dappled sunshine amongst trees. They grow up to 3 ft (92 cm) tall at the shoulder and only the males have antlers. The breeding period is in the autumn, when the males can be aggressive, and the young are born in early summer. Fallow deer will eat grass, nuts, and leaves and bark from trees.

4 For a short-cut back to Knole House continue along the road, but to complete the full route via Godden Green turn right off the road in front of a circular clump of small oak trees and follow the grassy track down

The pretty red and black cinnabar moth is often mistaken for a butterfly as it flies during the day, with a weak, fluttering flight. The caterpillars are also brightly coloured, with hoops of yellow and black around the body. This indicates to birds that, like the adults, they are distasteful and allows them to feed openly on ragwort plants, which they can reduce to a skeleton. In fact, they have been used to control this weed in Canada and New Zealand.

into a valley and up the steep slope on the other side. The path passes two dead tree trunks, the first 50 yards to the left and the next immediately alongside it. These are riddled with holes made by insect larvae and the woodpeckers that hunt for them. You may hear great spotted woodpeckers drumming on trees in the park and see green woodpeckers prospecting for ants on the grassland. Continue past a small pond on the right then keep to the left edge of a grassy area, before going between a tall oak and a beech to a gate in a fence to the right of a wooden gate.

5 Go straight on through the gate and on a path to reach a stone cottage after 100 yards. Go left up the road here between hedges of holly, elder, blackthorn and hazel, with gatekeeper and speckled wood butterflies flying along them. On reaching a T-junction with a track go left on it to soon reach a gravel road alongside cottages. Keep on to a parking area on the left and stone cottage on the right. To visit the pub at Godden Green turn right on a path between the stone cottage and riding stables for 250 yards to a road, then right (later retracing your steps).

6 To continue the walk take a path opposite the stone cottage, going between the gardens of bungalows and through a gate into a wood with silver birch trees and bushes of yellow-flowered broom. After 200 yards go left on a wider sandy cross-track and continue through the wood, with mauve rhododendrons colourful in spring. Soon there are fine views to the North Downs on the right, then you re-enter Knole Park through a gate and continue on a tarmac road. Just before the road crosses another golf fairway, you may spot a large plant of deadly nightshade with its poisonous black berries. Continue on a track between an avenue of oak trees, the Duchess Walk, back to Knole House. To return to Sevenoaks turn right on a road at the end of the tree avenue and follow it as it bends left past 'No Exit' signs. It goes downhill then, as it levels off, just past a large sweet chestnut tree on the left, go right on a sandy track to cross a valley and continue back up the path to the car park.

PLACE OF INTEREST NEARBY

Knole House (National Trust) is one of the largest mansions in the country, and dates from the 15th century. It has magnificent staterooms with four-poster beds and fine furniture, some made of silver. Telephone: 01732 450608.

WALK 4

HAYSDEN LAKE, LEIGH AND THE RIVER MEDWAY

– *lakes, woods and riverside*

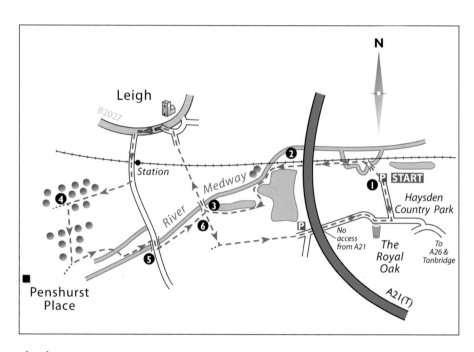

*T*he first part of this walk takes you past various watery habitats, including lakes that attract a variety of water birds such as great crested grebes and Canada geese. Later it goes through pleasant countryside and woodland that is colourful with wild flowers in spring, including bluebells, lady's smock and wild garlic. You are also likely to see butterflies such as orange tip, peacock and speckled wood, and water birds and plants may be observed during the section alongside the River Medway. There is the opportunity for a midway pub stop in the village of Leigh.

The route can be shortened by some 3¹/₂ miles by omitting Points 4 and 5 but you would miss out on some lovely views across the Weald.

THE WALK

1 From the western end of the car park (the far left end as you drive in) look for a sign saying 'footbridge to Haysden' and cross a footbridge over the river. Keep straight ahead on a gravel path, staying on this side of a railway line and walking parallel to it. There are sallows (pussy willows) and blackthorn bushes, with beneath them the mauve flowers of ground ivy and taller clumps of purple-flowered comfrey. Cross another footbridge to a T-junction with another path and turn left, then almost immediately right, signposted 'Haysden Lake', to continue alongside the railway (don't go under it). Go through a gap in a wooden fence and straight ahead up a short slope then down steps, to soon pass under a road viaduct. In the scrub on the right are wild cherry trees, with lovely white blossom in spring and vivid red leaf colours in autumn.

2 The path continues along the north edge of a lake, which has mallard, grebes and other water birds. About 100 yards past the

STARTING POINT: At the car park in Haysden Country Park. The longer walk could also be joined from Leigh village or railway station.

HOW TO GET THERE: Haysden Country Park is 1 mile west of Tonbridge and can be reached from the A26. Going south from Tonbridge, turn right from the A26 into Brook Street, past West Kent College, and take a right fork into Lower Haysden Lane to follow signs to the park. There are frequent bus services operated by Arriva along the A26, dropping you 1 mile from the start. Leigh is served by New Enterprise buses from Tonbridge and trains between Tonbridge and Redhill.

PARKING: In the large car park at Haysden Country Park.

REFRESHMENTS: The Royal Oak in Lower Haysden is close to the entrance to the country park and serves a good selection of food and drink. Telephone: 01732 350208. There are also pubs to be found in the village of Leigh.

LENGTH OF WALK: 6½ or 3 miles. Map: OS Explorer 147 Sevenoaks & Tonbridge (GR 572458).

viaduct take the left fork in the stony path to veer away from the railway and continue with the lake on the left and the river on the right, both with wild flowers on the banks and dragonflies and damselflies hovering over the water. Where the path forks again near a bench take the left fork near to the lake. Go through scrub colourful with wood anemones, celandines and lady's smock in spring, cross a footbridge, and turn sharp right. There is now a straight section between trees, with water on both sides. The lake seen through trees on the right often has Canada, greylag and Brent geese and great crested grebes nest there. There are also more flowers such as yellow archangel and greater stitchwort to be seen.

3 At a wooden marker post in the centre of the path turn left for the shorter walk, following the directions from Point 6 once at the stile. For the longer walk turn right over a stream then left to cross a footbridge. Go straight across a field and continue on a track under the railway to a kissing gate, then between houses to reach Leigh village green, and diagonally left across it to a main road. Turn left alongside the road, passing a shop and pubs. Just past the Fleur de Lys pub turn left along a road that passes Leigh railway station. **Take extreme care** as you walk under the railway bridge and uphill past a converted oasthouse as there is no footpath. Where the road bends left take a path on the right next to the entrance to Pauls Hill House. There is a wooden fence on the left and to the right lovely views across to

The great crested grebe almost became extinct in Britain in the mid-19th century, due to the fashion for using its feathers on ladies' hats. Fortunately, the populations have recovered and these beautiful birds are now a reasonably common sight on lakes and flooded gravel pits. The lovely chestnut colour of the ruff around the head is particularly evident during the breeding season in spring, when the male and female indulge in an amazing display, shaking their heads vigorously and rising out of the water together. They dive for their fish and invertebrate prey, often re-emerging at the surface a long distance away.

The starry white flowers of wood anemone make a wonderful sight as they carpet the floor of woods in March and April, before the trees leaf out and shade them. Any breeze will cause the dainty, pink-tinged flowers to move, giving them the alternative name of 'windflower'. They only open fully in full sunshine. The plant spreads rapidly by underground rhizomes and its presence indicates that the wood has been there for a long time.

the Greensand Ridge through trees with bluebells flowering in spring. Cross a stile next to a gate and at the next marker post go slightly left away from the fence to a stile at the far left corner of the narrow field, next to a large oak tree. Continue between an avenue of plane trees, with characteristic peeling bark and bobbles of seeds. Behind them are coppiced woods of sweet chestnut on the left, with silver birch and conifers on the right.

4 Go through a stile by a metal gate, then 70 yards on turn left at a marker post on the left. Keep to the left edge of a field, going gradually downhill with fine views to Penshurst Place and church ahead to the right. The path goes through a strip of woodland, then between another avenue of trees. About 200 yards before a house ahead go left at a stile in the fence on the left, next to a metal gate, and follow the estate road to two cottages. You are now on the Eden Valley Walk footpath. Just past the cottages leave the road at a stile on the right and go diagonally right down a field to a footbridge over a channel of the river, where aquatic plants can be seen. Continue to the bank of the River Medway and turn left to follow it to a road.

5 Turn right over a bridge and cross the road to a stile by a footpath sign. This path has a hedge on the left containing elder, hazel, sallow and blackthorn, providing flowers for insects in spring and fruits for birds in autumn and winter. Notice also the yellow lichens growing on the bark. The path continues under overhanging trees, where you can smell the wild garlic or ramsons growing here, with its white, star-shaped flowers and pungent leaves. There are also lots of wood anemones and lady's smock. The latter is a foodplant for the orange-tip butterfly and you may see the lovely males, with bright orange tips to the white wings, in April and May.

6 At a wooden post in the centre of the path turn right. Go over a stile then straight ahead down a field (not to the right) to a stile in the fence at the far end. Continue slightly left across the next field to another stile, then go sharp left, cross a stream after 100 yards, then across a field to a wooden pedestrian gate. Continue between hedges to a minor road near a car park and keep straight on along it for ¼ mile to the Royal Oak pub. Turn left along the road here to the entrance to the country park.

PLACES OF INTEREST NEARBY

There are boat trips along the river from the **Haysden Country Park**, which also has an adventure playground. **Tonbridge Castle** has a splendid 13th century gatehouse set in landscaped gardens alongside the River Medway in the centre of Tonbridge and can also be reached by boat from Haysden. Telephone: 01732 770929. **Penshurst Place** is a magnificent 14th century mansion with medieval great hall, staterooms, lovely gardens and adventure playground. Five miles south-west of Tonbridge; take the B2176 from the A26. Telephone: 01892 870307.

RYARSH WOOD, THE COLDRUM STONES AND THE NORTH DOWNS

– flowers of hedgebank, woods and downs

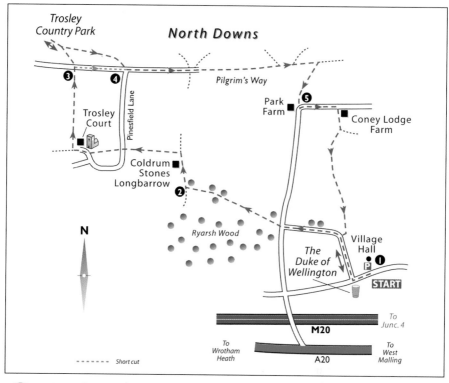

tarting along a lane whose banks are colourful with wild flowers, the walk then takes you through woods that are carpeted with bluebells, wood anemones and violets in spring. Later you pass an important Neolithic burial site and walk gradually up to the North Downs. There you have the option of a more strenuous climb to see the wonderful summertime array of wild flowers, including orchids, on the chalk downland. There are also lovely butterflies there, including vivid blues and the spectacular dark green fritillary. In addition, there are marvellous views over the countryside below. After a stretch along the ancient Pilgrims' Way you return through pleasant countryside, with woods and streams.

THE WALK

1 From the car park, with your back to the village hall, turn right alongside the road. After 150 yards, turn right opposite the pub to walk up Chapel Street. As the houses end follow the lane as it bends left, with banks that have celandines, stitchwort and germander speedwell in spring and tufted vetch in summer. Pass a small wood, white with wood anemones in spring, and continue to a T-junction. Go straight across to enter a wood at a stile. There are bluebells and wood anemones in spring and a good variety of trees, including wild cherry and hornbeam. The path, which can be muddy in places, leaves the wood at a plank bridge over a stream. After 30 yards take the stile on the right and continue through an area of recently planted trees of oak, birch, alder, cherry and whitebeam. In summer there is the purple of rosebay and great willowherb here and the yellow of bird's-foot trefoil, fleabane and meadow vetchling. Continue through a gap in a fence and straight on into another wood. In spring there is pink lady's smock in a meadow on the left and primroses bloom in the wood. Leave the wood at a stile and go straight across a field to another at the left corner of a clump of trees, then along the left edge of the trees to another stile.

STARTING POINT: In the village of Ryarsh, at the village hall.

HOW TO GET THERE: Ryarsh is just off the A20, 1 mile west of West Malling. From junction 4 of the M20 go south to the A20 then right (west) for 1 mile. Take a right turn signposted to Ryarsh, turning right at the first crossroads,

then straight on to reach the pub and village hall. Nu-Venture buses run from Maidstone to Ryarsh.

PARKING: In the car park at Ryarsh village hall.

REFRESHMENTS: The Duke of Wellington pub, which is near the car park, serves a good selection of food and drink in its comfortable dining room or large garden. Telephone: 01732 842318

LENGTH OF WALK: $5\frac{1}{4}$ miles. Map: OS Explorer 148 Maidstone & the Medway Towns (GR 671600).

2 Turn right onto a track, then where it forks after 80 yards keep right on a narrower path, often crossed by pheasants. Continue in the same direction on a concrete track past the Coldrum Stones longbarrow and keep straight on where the track bends right. Go past tall ash trees on the left and where the path forks after 100 yards go left. This path goes between fields, then with a hedge on the left, to reach a wide stony track which takes you to a minor road. Go straight across and on a path across a field to reach a lane by Trottiscliffe church. Turn right past the church and go through a wooden gate (marked private) into Trosley Court. Keep straight on between farm buildings, then just before the last barn on the right turn right to go past a marker post and climb gradually up to the North Downs between fields, then hedges, to reach the Pilgrims' Way road.

3 To avoid climbs turn right along the road to reach Point 4. However, if you have the energy it is well worth exploring the Downs here. Go up steps opposite, through a gate, and straight up the slope for 50 yards, then through a gate on the left to reach a large steep slope, part of Trosley Country Park. Here there is a wonderful profusion of colourful chalkland flowers

The exquisite deep blue flowers of germander speedwell colour hedgebanks, road verges and open grassland areas in spring and early summer. The white centres to the flowers have led to their alternative names of bird's-eye or cat's-eye and they were once worn by travellers as a good luck charm.

in summer – yellow horseshoe vetch and yellow-wort, pink thyme and centaury, purple selfheal and stemless thistle, lilac scabious and vivid pink-red pyramidal orchid. It is also a haven for insects, with a constant chirruping of grasshoppers. In July, the lovely dark green fritillary butterflies (orange and black on their uppersides) glide over the turf and there are also common and chalkhill blues and red and black burnet moths searching for flowers. Bushes of wayfaring tree develop red berries in summer and warblers sing from the scrub. Retrace your steps to the gate by which you entered the slope, then keep straight ahead on a well-marked path that runs along the middle of the next slope, parallel to the road below. Go to the very far end of the open area to where it narrows, through a kissing gate, then after 80 yards turn right to regain the Pilgrims' Way road opposite Pinesfield Lane.

The magnificent dark green fritillary is one of the largest butterflies in Britain; in Kent it only occurs at a few places on the North Downs. The orange and black adults are a glorious sight as they glide over the grassland, searching for flowers or mates. They feed on flowers such as thistles and knapweeds in July, when the lovely undersides, with silver spangles on a dark green background, can be seen. The larvae feed on violets.

4 Continue along the Pilgrims' Way (ie turn left if coming from the slope) and notice the wild strawberry, violets and quaking grass on the bank. Where the road ends and becomes a narrow path continue straight on, soon under overhanging trees where fallen hazelnuts reveal the presence of grey squirrels. There are occasional blue bellflowers and the path widens out, still under trees, including the dark foliage of yews. Keep straight on at two marker posts, the second near a derelict brick building, then 350 yards on the path bends right then left. At the left bend take a sunken track between hedges on the right (no footpath sign at time of writing). The hedges of blackthorn and field maple are festooned with traveller's joy and bryony in summer.

5 On reaching a road by a barn go sharp left along a concrete track (marked 'Coney Lodge Private Road') and after 400 yards go right on a concrete track in front of a house. Opposite the last barn on the left, take a path on the right. Keep to the left edge of the field with a wood on the left and where this ends keep straight on through a gap in trees, then keep to the right edge of the next field. Go past a small wood on the right, pungent with wild garlic in spring, then straight on where the wood ends and across a field, before keeping to the right of another small wood. With a stream on the left keep straight on through a gap in a hedge before crossing the stream and continuing with it on your right. Where the stream ends keep straight on past a telegraph pole and follow the left edge of a field to a track by a garage. Turn right for 50 yards to a road then left to return to the pub and car park.

PLACE OF INTEREST NEARBY
Trosley Country Park covers 160 acres on the North Downs, with waymarked walks through woods and downland, visitor centre, picnic area and refreshment kiosk. By car, you can enter it 4 miles north-west of Ryarsh, off the A227 at Vigo Village. Telephone: 01732 823570.

TESTON AND THE MEDWAY VALLEY
– riverbank and water meadows

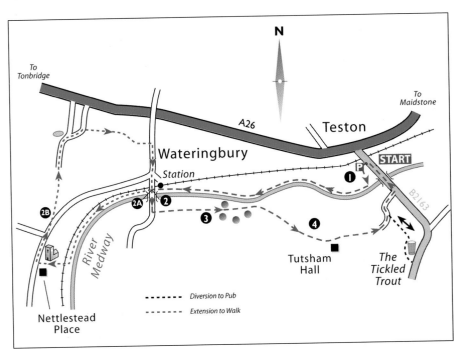

*T*his lovely riverside walk provides the opportunity to see colourful wetland flowers such as marsh marigolds and lady's smock in spring and a variety of dragonflies and damselflies in summer. The river has swans and mallard and you may see a heron, tern, or even a kingfisher hunting for fish. There is also a short stretch through a wood which is carpeted with bluebells, wood anemones and other brightly coloured flowers in spring.

The route can be extended by an extra 2 miles to take in a further stretch of riverside walking, and passes an ancient church, a medieval house and orchards. There are also some fine views along the valley.

THE WALK

1 From the car park of the picnic site head south across the meadow towards the river. Just before you reach it there is a small marshy area, which in spring is colourful with golden-yellow marsh marigolds or kingcups and pink lady's smock. At the riverbank turn right and follow it for a mile. On this stretch you will see lots of willows and alders, trees that like wet situations. Willows have elegant weeping branches and long narrow leaves which are fed on by many insects. Alders can be recognised by their characteristic brown seed cones and long catkins in spring. On the river you may see mute swans, Canada geese, mallards and possibly a heron or kingfisher if you are really lucky. Sometimes a black-headed gull or even a tern, with its forked tail, may fly over the water and there are martins in some places. Reed buntings can often be seen, while reed and sedge warblers are more often heard than seen. In

STARTING POINT: At Teston Bridge picnic site, owned by Kent County Council. The site has an adventure playground and a picnic area. If travelling by train the walk could also be joined at Wateringbury.

HOW TO GET THERE: Teston Bridge picnic site is 3 miles west of Maidstone, just off the A26. Travelling west, turn left on the B2163 and the entrance is just past a level crossing. Arriva buses between Maidstone and Tunbridge Wells run along the A26, a few hundred yards from the start. Wateringbury railway station (passed on the walk) is on the Maidstone West-Paddock Wood line.

PARKING: In the large car park at Teston Bridge picnic site (small charge).

REFRESHMENTS: The Tickled Trout pub at West Farleigh is 1 mile from Teston Bridge by road or can be reached on foot by a short diversion from the walk. It has a large family garden with play equipment (no children are allowed inside the pub in the evenings) and a wide choice of fish and meat dishes. Telephone: 01622 812589. Wateringbury village has a restaurant/ tearoom and a pub.

LENGTH OF WALK: 3 or 5 miles. Map: OS Explorer 148 Maidstone & the Medway Towns (GR 707533).

the summer, colourful dragonflies and damselflies patrol the riverside vegetation. Among the plants you will see are purple comfrey and yellow flag irises. You eventually reach a track running past moored boats. Follow this to a bridge near Wateringbury railway station and walk up the track to reach a road near to the old signal box. If you need refreshments the Riverside Restaurant on the other side of the road serves lunches and afternoon teas on most days from Easter to autumn, or there is the Railway Inn (open all day) across the level crossing.

2 For the longer walk follow the route from Point 2A (below). To continue the shorter walk turn left over the bridge across the river and 50 yards on go left at a stile with a Medway Valley Walk signpost. Cross another stile after 10 yards then go straight across another field that is yellow with buttercups in summer. Go through a kissing gate to another meadow that is managed under the Countryside Stewardship scheme. Keep to the left edge, with lady's smock in the wet meadow on the left, then keep slightly right from the next stile across another field to a wooden footbridge. To the left of the bridge notice the large nestbox on the tree, put there for the use of owls, such as the increasingly rare barn owl. Continue along the left edge of the next field to another footbridge and as you cross it look for the lovely blue flowers of brooklime alongside the stream in the summer months.

3 The path now enters a wood, which in spring is a blaze of colour with bluebells, yellow celandines and yellow archangel and the white of wood anemones and ramsons, the latter filling the air with the scent of garlic. You may hear a great spotted woodpecker drumming and the songs of willow warbler, blackcap, chaffinch and whitethroat. Grey squirrels use the branches as aerial walkways. Leave the wood at a stile then veer diagonally right away from the river, following a

*D*amselflies are the more delicate relations of dragonflies, from which they can be distinguished from the way they hold their wings along the back, rather than held out from the sides like an aeroplane. Damselflies often have lovely blue or metallic green colouring and hunt for small insects. The eggs are laid in aquatic plants and the nymphs live underwater, sometimes for several years, before becoming adult.

Looking like large buttercups, the bright yellow, shiny flowers of marsh marigolds, sometimes called kingcups, make a fine show in marshy areas and wet riverside meadows in spring. The leaves are a bright green but the whole plant is poisonous and animals avoid eating it. It can be abundant in some places, but overall it is in decline as wet areas are drained for agriculture or building.

line of yellow-topped wooden posts as you go gradually up a slope, with fine views to the left and back along the Medway Valley. Reach a stile by a corrugated iron barn with old apple trees behind it and continue on a stony track to farm buildings.

4 Just past a small stone barn on the left and just before the impressive Tutsham Hall on the right, go left at a stile and across grass to a narrow farm road winding gradually downhill. Continue past picturesque white-boarded cottages and an old millpond, then uphill past the massive trunks of ancient oak trees.

Where the road bends left there is the opportunity to visit a pub; this will add 3/4 mile to the walk. Turn right from the road over a stile and along the left edge of a long field. At its end go right for 30 yards then left through a gateway and straight up a field to a road opposite a Georgian mansion and with the Tickled Trout pub on your left. After your visit, retrace your steps to rejoin the walk.

Back at the bend in the road continue to follow it, with white garlic mustard and white deadnettle, vivid blue germander speedwell and alkanet, and mauve ground ivy on the hedgebank. You reach a T-junction with a busy road and need to **take extreme care** as you turn left along it as there is no footpath here or over the narrow medieval bridge. However, after this short section you are back at the picnic site.

2A To extend the walk from the bridge at Wateringbury (Point 2), instead of turning left over the bridge keep straight on alongside the river, past the Riverside Restaurant. Continue past caravans and over a footbridge, then past trees. Notice the fern-like leaves of hemlock, a poisonous plant looking similar to hedge parsley but with red spots on the stems. After $1/4$ mile, where the Medway Valley Path goes straight on at a marker post, go right over a stile and cross the railway line with care. Continue up the left side of a small field, over a stream, and past the garden of Nettlestead Place, a medieval manor house. Enter the churchyard of the lovely 15th century Nettlestead church, noticing the ancient yew trees, and turn left to walk alongside a stone wall with many ferns growing on it. On reaching a main road turn right and, on the opposite side, 30 yards past Gibbs Hill Road, go left on a tarmac footpath between hedges.

2B The path continues behind gardens to reach a metal barrier. Go left to another barrier, then along the right side of a field with a hedge containing hawthorn, ivy and elder on the right and with views along the Medway Valley. Pass a converted oasthouse and continue on a road, soon with a walled garden on the right. Look for mistletoe on the tall trees beyond it and for holly blue butterflies around the holly bushes. Follow the road as it bends right past a millpond with ducks and coot and where it forks keep right, then 50 yards on take a stony track on the right, opposite the weatherboarded Mill Oasthouse. The track passes apple and pear orchards, and after $1/2$ mile reaches a main road. Turn right to reach the Railway Inn and cross with care to the level crossing to resume the walk at Point 2.

PLACES OF INTEREST NEARBY
The Hop Farm Country Park has shire horses, a pets corner, a children's playground, exhibitions and a restaurant. It is 5 miles south-west of Teston, on the A228. Telephone: 01622 872068. **Yalding Organic Gardens** have gardens in various styles, all managed organically, plants and gifts, and a tearoom. At Yalding, 3 miles south of Teston. Telephone: 01622 814650.

WALK 7

BLUEBELL HILL AND BURHAM DOWN
– chalkland flowers and trees

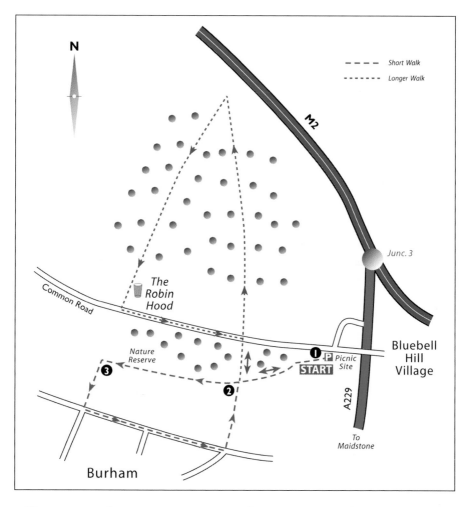

S tarting at the Kent County Council picnic site at Bluebell Hill, where there are spectacular views over the Medway Valley, the walk goes *over chalk downland and takes in the Kent Wildlife Trust nature reserve at Burham Down. Here the short turf has a profusion of wild flowers, including many orchids, and a variety of colourful butterflies. You will also see many different types of trees, including yew and whitebeam, and there is the opportunity to do a longer walk through bluebell woods.*

THE WALK

1 From the right hand end of the car park at the picnic site (with your back to the entrance) walk along the top path and through a wooden kissing gate. There are fine views over the Medway Valley and to the Greensand Ridge in the distance. In the short turf are characteristic flowers of the chalk downland and below is a large disused chalk quarry, where birds such as kestrels nest. Continue to the right of a wooden seat to another kissing gate, then turn left to go downhill on a footpath between a wire fence and a hedge, then under overhanging yew trees, to reach a short wooden barrier fence at a junction with another track.

STARTING POINT: The car park at the picnic site at Bluebell Hill.

HOW TO GET THERE: The picnic site is west of the A229 between Maidstone and Chatham at Bluebell Hill, near junction 3 of the M2 and junction 6 of the M20, and is reached by a slip road from the A229. Arriva buses between Maidstone and Chatham run a frequent service through Bluebell Hill village, 1/4 mile from the start, and also serve Burham village.

PARKING: In the car park at the Kent County Council picnic site at Bluebell Hill.

REFRESHMENTS: The Robin Hood pub is 3/4 mile from the starting point and is passed on the longer walk. It has a good selection of beers and food, with a separate dining area. There is a garden with a small playground and the added attraction of tame animals and an aviary. Telephone: 01634 861500.

LENGTH OF WALK: 2³/₄ or 5¹/₂ miles. Map: OS Explorer 148 Maidstone & the Medway Towns (GR 743622).

For the longer walk turn right here on a wide shale track that climbs up under the dark shade of more yews and reaches a minor road. Go straight across to a footpath by a metal gate, cross a field, then enter a wood by a metal barrier gate. The path goes along the left edge of a wood consisting mainly of sweet chestnut and colourful with bluebells in spring. Continue through the middle of a wood for 3/4 mile, always keeping straight on along the main path, which is wide at first but becomes narrow and is muddy in places. There are woodland flowers such as bugle, yellow pimpernel and wood spurge and the songs of birds like chiffchaff and chaffinch. The path eventually goes downhill through yew trees and leaves the wood at a stile. Continue towards the M2 motorway and Channel Tunnel rail link ahead, between newly-planted trees to another stile at a T-junction with another path. Turn sharp left away from the motorway to follow the path gradually uphill between hedges then through the right edge of a wood, with trees such as whitebeam and hornbeam. After 3/4 mile the path becomes narrower as it goes between tall hawthorn and hazel bushes to reach the Robin Hood pub. Continue to the minor road ahead, turn left for 400 yards, then turn right at the byway sign and rejoin the shorter walk at Point 2, where you turn right off the track.

The man orchid has one of the most unusual flowers, resembling a matchstick man wearing a large helmet. These individual flowers make up a longer spike, but man orchids are not easy to spot on the chalk grassland where they occur as they are mainly in shades of green and brown, though sometimes they have lovely red veining and edging. They flower in May and early June, but are very local in distribution.

2 For the shorter walk, go straight across the shale track to a narrow path between bushes and trees. As you continue you may see speckled wood, gatekeeper and brimstone butterflies and the trees and bushes include beech, whitebeam and holly, with flowers such as herb robert and herb bennet beneath. Ignore a footpath

The common blue, as befits its name, is the commonest of the blue butterflies in Britain, and can be found in large colonies at some sites, particularly on downland. Its caterpillars feed on bird's-foot trefoil and some related plants. The adult males have wings of a brilliant blue with a white fringe, while the females are usually less colourful, having dark brown wings with blue only near the body.

going off to the left and where the path forks 80 yards on take the right (upper) fork. When you reach a kissing gate on the right go through it into part of the Kent Wildlife Trust nature reserve of Burham Down. Keep to the main path near the bottom of the slope and continue in the same direction as formerly. The short turf here contains beautiful chalkland flowers such as blue and mauve milkwort and yellow horseshoe vetch. The latter is the foodplant of the caterpillars of the lovely milky-blue chalkhill blue butterfly which occurs here, as does the common blue, which is a brighter shade of blue. There are also orchids here, including the unusual man orchid in late May/early June, the fly orchid, and later in June/July pyramidal and common spotted orchids. The path eventually ends at another kissing gate. Go through it and maintain the same direction on a footpath, soon reaching a T-junction with a wide shale path.

3 Turn left on the track to go downhill between steep hedgebanks covered in ivy, beneath hedges of elder, hawthorn and wayfaring tree, to reach a road. Turn left and follow it through the village of Burham, which has a few pubs, including two down Church Road opposite, shops and a bakery. Continue for ½ mile until you reach Court Road on the right, then cross over the road to a track, signposted as a byway, next to a bus shelter. The track climbs gradually back up to the Downs, on the slopes of which you can see the contrast between the dark green of the yews and the pale whitish-green of the whitebeams. At the sides of the track are a profusion of wild flowers, at their best in May and June, including yellow-green crosswort, pink herb robert, vivid blue germander speedwell, yellow kidney vetch, bird's-foot trefoil and rock rose and white bladder campion, also more man orchids. The hedges contain privet, field maple, dogwood, hazel, wayfaring tree and spindle, with wild roses, bryony and honeysuckle twining through them. You may also see butterflies such as orange-tip, brimstone, peacock and common and holly blues. The path continues between trees to reach the wooden barrier fence on the right at Point 2. Turn right here to retrace your steps to the car park.

PLACES OF INTEREST NEARBY

Tyland Barn is a restored 17th century barn which houses the visitor centre of the Kent Wildlife Trust and has wildlife displays, natural history books and gifts, and an outdoor nature area. It is 1 mile south of Bluebell Hill and signposted from the A229. Telephone: 01622 662012. The **Museum of Kent Life** is an open air museum with historic buildings, farm animals and exhibitions. Off the A229 near junction 6 of the M20. Telephone: 01622 763936.

WALK 8

CAMER COUNTRY PARK, HENLEY WOOD AND LUDDESDOWN

– hedges, woods and flowers

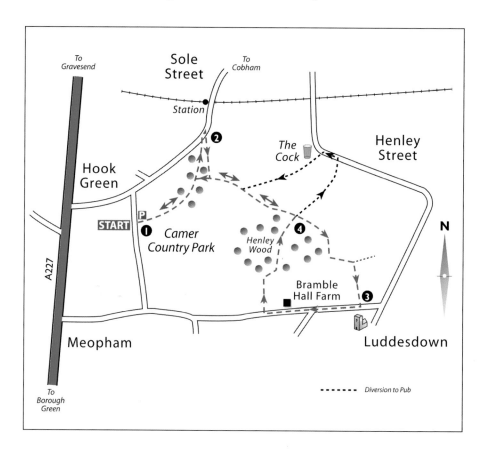

S *tarting at Camer Country Park, this walk goes through parkland with a fine variety of trees, then lovely rolling countryside on the top of the North Downs. It passes remnants of ancient woodland, grassland with a good variety of wild flowers and the fields of an organic farm, where you may see arable weeds that have been wiped out in most other places.*

THE WALK

1 From the kiosk at the country park, with your back to the side with the toilets, walk straight ahead past the right edge of the main car park on to the track coming from it. Keep to the left edge of a grass area with trees on the left and between tall sycamores and horse chestnuts. Continue along the left edge of another grassy area, with a children's playground 100 yards to the right, and a hedge of elder, field maple and hawthorn on the left. Keep left of a 100 ft tall redwood, with its spongy, fibrous bark, and along a stony path between an avenue of young lime trees, fragrant with blossom in summer. Follow this avenue to reach a road by a lodge.

2 After 5 yards go right down a shale track, part of the Wealdway long-distance footpath. There are wild hops in the hedge on the right and thistles and nettles alongside the track attract butterflies such as peacock and small tortoiseshell. Follow the track past houses, then a wood on the right where you may see or hear a jay. Keep straight on at a

STARTING POINT: At the car park at Camer Country Park, which has a small refreshment kiosk and a children's playground.

HOW TO GET THERE: From the A227 the turn-off to Camer Country Park is signposted at Hook Green, 1/2 mile north of Meopham, then after 1/4 mile turn right into Camer Park Road to reach the entrance.

Arriva buses from Gravesend run past the country park. The walk could also be joined from Sole Street railway station, a few hundred yards from Point 2.

PARKING: In the large car park at Camer Country Park.

REFRESHMENTS: The Cock Inn at Henley Street is situated 1½ miles from the country park by road, or the walk can be extended to visit it. It has a good choice of food and real ales and ciders, with comfortable bars and a pleasant garden. Telephone: 01474 814208

LENGTH OF WALK: 3½ miles. Map: OS Explorer 163 Gravesend & Rochester (GR 650668).

marker post where the wood ends and along the left edge of a field that has flowers such as centaury, betony, thyme, marjoram and selfheal. Enter a wood by a marker post and exit over a stile then turn right along the right edge of a field with woodland on the right which has spindle bushes carrying orange and pink fruits in autumn. You will often see pheasants here. Go down to a stile, down steps, then left along the top of a bank. There are fine views over the valley below and more chalkland flowers such as lady's bedstraw, mullein, St John's wort, scabious and bird's-foot trefoil. Go over another stile and 100 yards on turn right at a marker post to go downhill through a field. The fields around here are farmed organically, so it is a good place to see arable weeds that are now less common, such as poppies. Continue down a flowery bank and between fields to a road.

3 Go right along the road and keep right where it forks. Go past Bramble Hall Farm on the right, then where there are footpath signs on both sides of the road go right over a stile and up the left side of a field with flowers and lots of meadow brown butterflies in summer. Cross a stile at the top and go diagonally left through woodland. On the right the trees have been cleared, allowing flowers such as yellow mullein and blue nettle-leaved bellflower to flourish. On reaching a wider track on its bend turn sharp left on it to go through more trees, with goldenrod growing beneath. Continue with a wood on the left and a field on the right which has pyramidal orchids and pink centaury.

A s the small tortoiseshell is one of our commoner butterflies, the beauty of its colours is not always fully appreciated. It can often be seen feeding on flowers such as buddleia or sunbathing on the ground. The caterpillars, which are black with yellowish markings, live in large groups on nettles, making webs on the foliage. The adults often hibernate in houses or sheds, emerging to feed on sunny days in spring.

4 To extend the walk by ³/₄ mile and visit the pub, go left for 10 yards where the wood ends then right on a grassy track between fields, with lots of lovely blue flowers of chicory. Keep to the right of a hedgebank and on between tall ash trees to a road, then left to the pub. To complete the

The common or field poppy is one of the most famous weeds of cultivation. Its seeds can survive in the soil for decades, germinating only when disturbance provides light, as occurred on the battlefields of the First World War. Each plant can produce 17,000 seeds. Having become a rare sight, the lovely scarlet-red flowers are having something of a revival as the amount of organic and set-aside land increases.

loop turn right going out of the pub entrance, but immediately right again on a path alongside the pub grounds. Go past oak trees and a large field maple and along the left edge of a field, past wild cherry trees on the left and between banks topped by holly bushes. On reaching the wide stony track turn right to return to the country park or left if starting the walk from the pub.

For the 3½ mile circuit, not including the pub at Henley Street, go left where the wood ends at Point 4. You are now retracing your steps from the outward journey, so are soon back on the shale track leading back to the country park. Where this track eventually bends right (by telegraph pole no 429 with several yellow arrows on it) take a short-cut into the country park by going straight on past a wooden barrier fence. Continue straight on through trees, past a large oak tree, and straight across a field to reach the avenue of lime trees. Turn left on the track to return to the car park.

PLACE OF INTEREST NEARBY

Cobham Hall is a large mansion dating from 1584, with lovely interiors. It is now a school but open to the public during the holidays. In Cobham, 2 miles north-east of Camer. Telephone: 01474 823371.

WALK 9

NORTHWARD HILL AND
THE RIVER THAMES

– woods, river and marsh

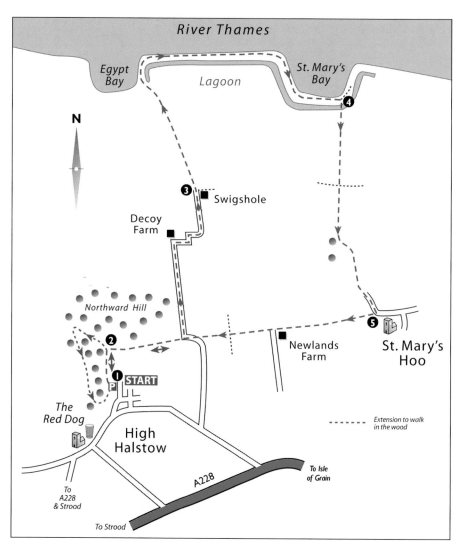

*I*t is well worth taking binoculars on this walk as you pass some wonderful bird watching sites, including the largest heronry in the country. There are many other birds to see and hear in the ancient woodland where the walk starts, including nightingales and turtle doves, as well as rare butterflies and colourful wild flowers. Later you walk alongside the wide River Thames and there are many types of waders and wildfowl to observe on the mudflats of the river and on the marshes inland, where birds of prey such as owls and harriers may be seen hunting. In summer, brightly-coloured dragonflies abound over the drainage ditches. Although this is one of the longer walks it is mainly flat. There are also shorter colour-coded, RSPB waymarked walks around the reserve from the car park.

THE WALK

1 From the RSPB car park go through a gate opposite garages into the wood, down steps and ahead on the path. Alongside are the yellow daisy-like flowers of fleabane, which attract meadow brown and gatekeeper butterflies. At a T-junction with another path go right up a gradual slope and follow the path as it bends left behind houses. There

STARTING POINT: At the car park of the RSPB's Northward Hill nature reserve.

HOW TO GET THERE: High Halstow is 6 miles north-east of Strood and reached on a minor road from the A228. At a T-junction in front of the pub in the village turn right, then after 1/4 mile left into Longfield Avenue. Go first left into Harrison Drive and turn

right into Northward Avenue, with the car park shortly on the left. Arriva buses run from the Medway towns to High Halstow.

PARKING: In the RSPB car park off Northward Avenue.

REFRESHMENTS: The Red Dog pub is in the centre of High Halstow village, 1/4 mile from the start, and provides a selection of food and ales. Telephone: 01634 250336.

LENGTH OF WALK: 7 1/2 or 8 1/2 miles. Map: OS Explorer 163 Gravesend & Rochester (GR 782757).

are large oak trees here, which may have purple hairstreak butterflies flying around the foliage. Listen for the songs of nightingales and warblers. At a marker post on the right keep straight on, with bluebells in the woods in spring, and where the path forks at the next marker post go right up shallow steps. There are lots of small elm trees here and they provide food for the caterpillars of the rare white-letter hairstreak butterfly. The path bends left by a large oak tree with adjacent gate and after 15 yards reaches a broader, stony cross-track.

2 This is the Saxon Shore Way footpath – go right on it to a kissing gate after 20 yards, then left at a marker post and along the left edge of a field, with blackthorn scrub on the left. At the corner of the field go through a gap in the hedge, straight across a field, then along the left edge of the next field, with a ditch and later dead elms on the left, to reach a minor road. Turn left and follow the road, with yarrow and herb robert on the banks. Continue through bends and later past damson trees on the right to where the road ends at Swigshole Cottage.

3 Continue straight ahead on a wide track to a T-junction with another track and turn left. The track has rushes on the right and teasels that attract immigrant butterflies such as painted lady and clouded yellow. About 20 yards before a metal gate across the track go left over a double stile, then diagonally right across a field with thistles to another stile and on to a raised bank. Turn right along the bank, with the dyke below home to many dragonflies, to reach the 'sea wall' alongside the River Thames. Turn right along the raised bank, with views across to the Essex shore. The lagoon below is a good place for seeing swans and various ducks such as teal and wigeon, while in the fields beyond it

G rey herons are usually seen near water, often standing motionless before striking quickly with their long dagger-like beak to spear a fish. The drainage ditches of the North Kent marshes provide an ideal habitat and they nest nearby in the tall trees on Northward Hill, where there may be as many as 200 pairs. They are noisy and aggressive on the large tree-top nest, made of sticks and used every year. In flight a heron conjures up images of a pterodactyl, with its broad flapping wings and long legs trailing behind.

flocks of lapwing and golden plover feed in winter. On the mudflats at the side of the river shelduck, dunlin and knot often feed. Continue for 1 mile past several metal gates to an inlet, with a marshy area on the left that has yellow flowers of golden samphire and lilac sea aster and sea lavender. The flowers attract migrant butterflies such as the painted lady.

*W**hen you see the pretty painted lady butterfly in Kent it may have travelled hundreds of miles to get there, as it migrates north from North Africa and southern Europe. Because of this, numbers reaching our shores fluctuate tremendously from year to year. When they arrive they need to replenish their energy, so can sometimes be seen in large numbers feeding on the nectar of flowers near the coast.*

4 Where the bank swings sharp left at the end of the marshy area go right to a track between lagoons to a gate and stile, then straight on with a rush-filled dyke on the left providing ideal habitat for reed and sedge warblers. Look out for herons fishing. When the track bends right go straight on past a wooden gate to a stile, then slightly diagonally left, aiming for a clump of trees on the horizon, to a stile near a double wooden gate. Continue straight on to a stile just to the left of the trees, then diagonally left on a rough tarmac track. At a cross-track go left on it and continue as it bends right.

5 On reaching houses and a road that bends left to a church go right on the bend on a stony track and keep straight on where it ends, to follow a line of telegraph poles along the left edge of a field. Opposite a long stone building on the left and just after a corrugated metal barn on the right go up steps and to the right of a pond, then on a grassy track between fields. Keep straight on where a path crosses to soon reach a road, with swallows swooping overhead. Go straight on along the road and just after it bends right go left on a footpath to retrace your footsteps to the woods by continuing to a gap in a hedge, then along the right edge of a field to a marker post.

Go right into the wood here and straight on along a stony track. For the direct route back to the car park turn left at the marker post after 20 yards (Point 2). To explore the nature reserve keep straight on past blackthorn scrub, later with the heronry on the right, and under oak trees to a more open area with gorse bushes. Follow the path as it goes gradually downhill, then at a short marker post with a green arrow on the left turn left. You follow the green arrow markers on the path as it goes through the wood and elm scrub to eventually reach a concrete cross-track. Turn left on this to return to the car park.

PLACE OF INTEREST NEARBY
Rochester Castle has one of the tallest keeps in England, a fine example of Norman architecture. Situated next to the River Medway in Rochester, 5 miles south-west of High Halstow. Telephone: 01634 402276.

CRANBROOK AND ITS WEALDEN WOODS

– woods and streams

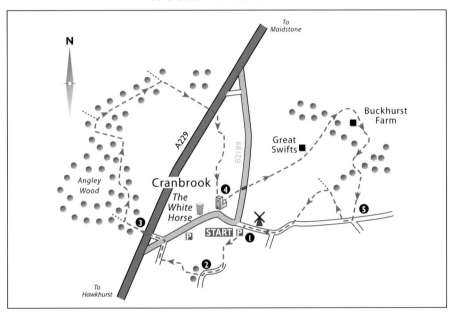

The small town of Cranbrook, which forms the starting point for this walk, has some fine buildings including an impressive church and a fine smock windmill which is still in working order. The walk is in two loops, on either side of the town, so could be done in one go or as two separate walks. The first part goes through Angley Wood, where there are fine displays of bluebells and other flowers in spring. After returning to Cranbrook, the second part goes through pleasant countryside and small woods, crossing several gurgling streams, and past banks of violets and primroses. Children will enjoy the natural playground of trees in Angley Wood and the footbridges over the streams.

THE WALK

1 Walk to the end of the car park furthest from the entrance and take a path to the left of a stream, with houses on the left. Go past a cul-desac on the left and just before a scout hut go left on a path behind gardens. The path goes between tall hedges, with yellow celandines and pink herb robert below. On reaching a suburban road continue for 15 yards then turn right down a narrow lane. On the left is an old apple orchard with sheep grazing beneath, a rare sight nowadays. There are many flowers on the bank on the right, including in spring white stitchwort and wood anemones, blue germander speedwell and bluebells.

2 Where the lane bends left keep straight on into a small wood with carpets of wood anemones, celandines and bluebells and an understorey of holly. Leave it by a stile and keep to the right edge of a field with another flower-rich wood on the right. Ignore a stile into the wood and continue until the trees on the right end, then go right to a stile and cross a stream by a plank bridge. Go left to a stile after 10 yards then right to another after 50 yards and straight across a small field and over another stile near a large oak tree. Go sharp left here to reach a track road and go right to a wider road. Cross it and continue on a road between houses to a main road.

3 Cross the road with care to enter a wood by a metal gate. There are often orange tip butterflies here in May. Walk on the track between

STARTING POINT: At the public car park off The Hill in Cranbrook.

HOW TO GET THERE: Cranbrook is on the A229 between Maidstone and Hawkhurst. Travelling south from Maidstone turn left off the A229 on the B2189 into the town and left at a T-junction into The Hill, with

the car park almost immediately on the right. Cranbrook is served by Arriva buses from Maidstone and Tunbridge Wells.

PARKING: In the public car park off The Hill. If full, there is another public car park off the High Street.

REFRESHMENTS: Cranbrook has several pubs, a tearoom and coffee shop. The White Horse, in the High Street near the church, is a Victorian pub with a restaurant. Telephone: 01580 712625.

LENGTH OF WALK: 6 miles (can be done in 2 loops of 3 miles). Map: OS Explorer 136 The Weald (GR 778359).

trees, going right where it forks by a wooden post saying 'High Weald Landscape Trail'. Continue on the wide sandy track between coppiced sweet chestnut trees, keeping straight on where another path leaves on the left, then a little further on take the right fork. There are now conifers and birch trees – notice how little vegetation grows beneath the conifers. However, some birds such as goldcrests, coal tits and crossbills favour them. Soon fields are visible through the trees on the right. Keep to the main track as it swings left, with heather and bracken revealing the acidic nature of the soil. At a marker post with yellow arrow follow the track sharp left and keep straight on at the next post, then at a third post, at the base of a large beech tree, bear diagonally right over a stream. Notice the rust-coloured water, the result of iron being leached from the soil. Take the right fork in the path 20 yards on at a marker post to cross another bridge by the garden of an old farmhouse. The path continues uphill between birch, holly, and rhododendron and is muddy in places. Keep straight on through more sweet chestnut coppice, eventually with a wire fence on the right, then horse paddocks. Look for bracket fungi on the birches and you may hear a woodpecker drumming and see parties of blue or long-tailed tits flitting through the trees. Continue until a main road is reached near a rugby field. Cross carefully to a narrow path between houses then go straight across a meadow before bearing right through a wooden gate and on between school grounds. On reaching a suburban road turn sharp left on a path between houses which leads to a church-yard. If you want to return to the car park at this point continue through the church-yard and left on the road.

4 To continue the walk turn left along the churchyard wall, noticing the fine lime trees bordering it, then along the right edge of a sports field to reach a road. Go straight across to a path, with fine parkland trees behind a fence on the left, and continue as it becomes a concrete track with stately oak trees on the left. Where the track swings right go left at a stile into a wood with holly, honeysuckle and tall beech trees. The path goes

A butterfly that is truly a harbinger of spring, the orange tip usually appears in April, with peak numbers in May. Only the male has the bright orange tips to the white wings; those of the female are grey-black. Both sexes have a lovely mottled green pattern on the undersides of the wings, providing wonderful camouflage when resting on vegetation. Their caterpillars feed on the seedpods of garlic mustard and lady's smock.

The early purple is one of the first orchids to appear, flowering in damp woods and on downland in spring. The flowers are lovely shades of pink and purple and the leaves are usually heavily spotted with dark blotches. This orchid looks particularly attractive when seen with bluebells or cowslips, but unfortunately it occurs in fewer places then it used to.

downhill with wood anemones, bluebells and primroses alongside. Leave the wood over a stile and go straight up a field to another stile and down steps to a lane. Turn right and just before the first farm building on the left go left at a concrete footpath sign on a path that soon reaches a farm road. Go left and follow the road as it bends right and later passes a small wood. Continue past a metal barn and cottages then through trees with lady's smock and bugle beneath. As you cross a stream notice yellow archangel and ramsons on the right and as the road continues there are violets and primroses on the banks and bushes of broom.

5 On reaching a T-junction with a minor road go right for 100 yards then right at a stile opposite a large timbered house. Cross a field to a gap in a tall hedge and continue with trees on the right, under which a variety of flowers bloom in spring, including bluebells, moschatel, wood anemones and early purple orchids. Cross a stream by a foot-bridge then 20 yards on turn sharp left. At a metal marker post turn left to re-cross the stream and follow the right edge of a field, with hawthorns and other trees on the right. Just before the end of the field go down to a stile on the right then turn left on a concrete track to soon reach a road. Turn right to walk alongside the road to return to the car park.

PLACES OF INTEREST NEARBY
Union Windmill in Cranbrook is the largest smock mill in the county and is open with demonstrations on summer Saturdays and some Sundays. Telephone: 01580 712256. **Sissinghurst Castle Garden** (National Trust) is a delightful, world-renowned garden, created around the ruins of a large Elizabethan house. It is located 2 miles north-east of Cranbrook, off the A262. Telephone: 01580 710701.

CHARING AND WESTWELL DOWNS

– *wood anemones and woodpeckers*

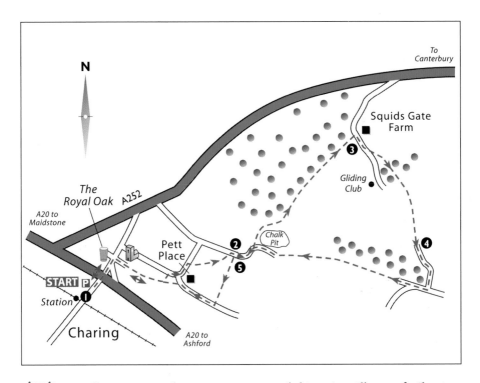

*T*his walk starts in the picturesque and historic village of Charing, with its ancient church and remains of an archbishop's palace. After passing these it goes through pleasant countryside to an area of mixed woodland. Here there are carpets of bluebells, violets, wood anemones and celandines in spring and the singing of many woodland birds. The woods were badly damaged in the 1987 storm, but have recovered well and the dead trees provide a habitat for woodpeckers. You are also likely to see butterflies such as the lovely lemon-yellow brimstone, and there are fabulous views over the countryside below the Downs. The walk includes a gradual climb up the Downs.

THE WALK

1 From the entrance to the car park turn left to the junction with the A20 and go straight across and up the main village street, with the Royal Oak on the left. Take the second on the right, Market Place, which goes past a library, then the remains of the ancient archbishop's palace. Take the path to the right of the church, along an alley between fences, then the left edge of a playing field to a wooden gate. Keep to the left edge of the next field, where the beds of nettles provide food for the caterpillars of peacock and small tortoiseshell butterflies, often seen here. Where the hedge on the left, with starry white blackthorn blossom in spring, ends continue straight on across a field to a stile, but turn left before it to reach a minor road. Turn right on it, but soon take a lane on the left. There are views to the Downs and a windmill on the left and the bank on the right has violets and other flowers. After 200 yards go up steps on the right to a stile and diagonally left across a large field. (If the field is muddy the alternative is to stay on the lane and turn right at a T-junction to reach Point 2.)

2 At the far left corner of the field go over a stile to a minor road and turn right. Follow the road as it bends left past a white house, then

STARTING POINT: At the public car park just south of the A20 in Charing village.

HOW TO GET THERE: Charing is at the junction of the A20 and the A252, 6 miles north-west of Ashford. Travelling on the A20 from Ashford, turn left at the crossroads in the village into Station Road and the car park is shortly on the right. Charing is served by buses (Stagecoach-East Kent) and trains between Maidstone and Ashford.

PARKING: In the public car park south of the A20 in Charing.

REFRESHMENTS: There is a choice of pubs and a good restaurant/tearoom in Charing. The Royal Oak offers a wide range of food in pleasant surroundings. Telephone: 01233 712612.

LENGTH OF WALK: 6³/₄ miles. Map: OS Explorer 137 Ashford (GR 952493).

as it bends right go straight ahead on a track going up through the edge of a wood, with a garden on the left. The track climbs gradually uphill between banks that are colourful with flowers in spring. There are primroses, violets, wild strawberry and the delicate white flowers of wood sorrel, veined with mauve. As the track reaches the top of the slope there are sheets of white wood anemones beneath the trees. Continue with a gliding club field on the right, where you can watch the planes soar above the singing skylarks. In the wood on the left there are carpets of wood anemones and bluebells in April and May. A pretty day-flying moth, the orange underwing, may land on the path, or a beautiful lemon-yellow brimstone butterfly fly along the woodland edge.

3 On reaching a minor road turn right. After 400 yards go left over a stile opposite a footpath sign. If you need refreshments at this point continue along the road to the café at the gliding club, open most weekends. To avoid stiles or allergy problems with oilseed rape you could continue along the road past the gliding club and rejoin the route at Point 4. From the stile go diagonally right across a field, to the right of the right hand telegraph pole, to a stile into a wood which has lots of grey squirrels. Keep straight on, ignoring any cross-paths, to a stile at the end of the wood. Continue straight on through an arable field, keeping left of a small pond and straight on where another path goes off left. After another stile aim to the right of the right edge of a wood ahead, with fine views ahead to the Greensand Ridge in the distance. Cross a small field via stiles at either end, then go straight down a long field to the far corner, where it narrows to a point. Go through a metal gate and after 30 yards turn left on a metalled track (the continuation of the road past the gliding club).

4 Alongside the track are sheets of yellow celandines in spring, and the unusual moschatel, whose lime-green flowers are arranged as four around the stem with another on top,

The shiny, bright yellow flowers of lesser celandine make a glorious sight as they make starry carpets in damp woodland and on hedgebanks in spring. The flowers only open in bright sun, but may be seen as early as February or occasionally even January. The leaves are heart-shaped and the plants spread rapidly.

The lovely brimstone butterfly is one of the first to appear in spring. The male is a brighter yellow than the pale lemon-yellow female, and may be the 'butter-coloured fly' from which the term butterfly may derive. When its wings are closed the wings of the brimstone appear leaf-shaped, providing excellent camouflage when resting amongst vegetation. It is most likely to be seen near woodland on the Downs but can occur almost anywhere.

giving it the alternative name of town hall clock. Go past houses and continue between hedgebanks adorned with primroses to a T-junction, then turn right along the Pilgrims' Way. After 250 yards take the right fork then keep on the main, left hand track past houses, and soon with views through a narrow strip of trees on the left. The woods on the right suffered severe damage in the 1987 storm and there are reminders in the form of uprooted trees and others that are skeletal and pock-marked with holes made by insects and the woodpeckers prospecting for them. However, the woods are regenerating well and are alive with the sound of birds such as warblers, chaffinch and whitethroat. In spring the unfolding young leaves of the beech trees are a lovely green against a blue sky, and speckled wood butterflies bask in the dappled sunshine. The track eventually becomes a road, taking you past a chalk quarry on the right and back to your outward route.

5 Keep on the road, but about 100 yards past the white house turn left at a large tree with a hidden byway sign to go down a sunken track between tall hedges of hazel, hawthorn and blackthorn. On reaching a minor road turn right, with flowers such as white stitchwort and blue speedwell on the bank. At a bend just past the impressive Pett Place cross a stile on the left and keep straight on to return to Charing church and village.

PLACE OF INTEREST NEARBY
Beech Court Gardens have magnificent trees, spacious lawns and displays of azaleas and rhododendrons. At Challock, 3 miles east of Charing, just off the A252. Telephone: 01233 740735.

WALK 12

HOTHFIELD COMMON AND THE STOUR VALLEY

– *heather and hedges*

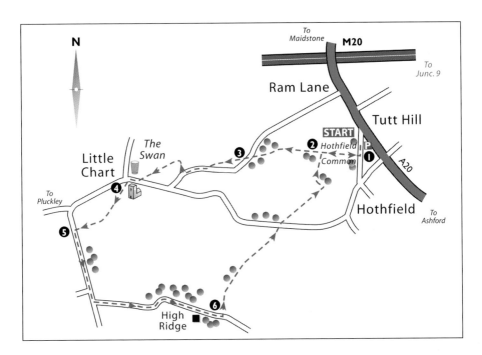

*H*othfield Common, where the walk starts, is a rare type of habitat for Kent, an acid bog. Here you can see plants that hardly occur elsewhere in the county, such as bog asphodel, sundew and heath spotted orchid. Heather and cross-leaved heath make pink and purple carpets in late summer and colourful dragonflies and damselflies can be seen here and elsewhere on the walk. Later you go through picturesque countryside with streams, orchards and woods, with a section along quiet lanes.

THE WALK

1 Going out of the car park entrance, turn left along the road for 200 yards then go right at a Greensand Way footpath sign to enter a

59

wood by a metal barrier and information board. Keep straight ahead through trees, noting the unusual acorns of a Turkey oak, then straight on with English oaks on the left and ahead on a grassy path through bracken. This illustrates the acidic nature of the soil on Hothfield Common, allowing plants such as heather and cross-leaved heath to flourish. Where the path forks, 150 yards out of the trees, keep left. A little further on, four paths diverge – take the far right one to walk through a clump of birch trees.

2 Past the trees look for a short post with Greensand Way and Stour Valley Walk markers on the side and go straight on to the left of it on a path which leads into trees again. You will be following these long-distance path markers for the next part of the walk. Leave the trees at a stile and go straight ahead on a wide grassy path. Cross a stream and continue with it on the right, lined by alders and willows; you may see damselflies, including the lovely banded demoiselle. Keep to the right edge of the field, then by a tall lime tree on the right with a marker post hidden at its base keep straight on across the field to a footbridge over a stream and into a wood. The wood has bluebells in spring and foxgloves in summer. Continue through it to reach a minor road.

STARTING POINT: At the car park south of the A20 at Hothfield Common.

HOW TO GET THERE: Hothfield Common is 4 miles north-west of Ashford, off the A20. Travelling towards Maidstone, turn off left at the second turn signposted to Hothfield village (not the first). The car park is a few hundred yards on the left.

Stagecoach buses between Ashford and Maidstone stop at the edge of Hothfield village, a short distance from the start.

PARKING: In the public car park just south of the A20.

REFRESHMENTS: There are pubs a short distance north-west of the starting point, alongside the A20 at Tutt Hill. Alternatively, the Swan at Little Chart is a lovely country pub with a good choice of food. It is 2 miles from the start by road, but passed on the walk. Telephone: 01233 840702.

LENGTH OF WALK: 6¼ miles. Map: OS Explorer 137 Ashford (GR 972458).

3 Cross the road to a path across a field that will lead back to the road (if the field is muddy walk left along the road). Back on the road turn right and just past a cricket pitch turn right up a driveway at a footpath sign. Go past a large pond with ducks and where the drive ends by a thatched cottage go straight on for 50 yards then follow the grassy track as it bends left at the end of a garden. The hedge on the right has hawthorn, elder, elm and bramble, and gatekeeper butterflies fly along it. After a stile go along the left edge of a field to another stile, then slightly right to a section of electric fence with yellow insulation tape, then diagonally right to another taped section of fence. Continue straight on, aiming just to the left of a house ahead, to a stile by a gate and turn right on the road with care, then past a church to the Swan pub at Little Chart.

4 Opposite the pub sign in the car park go through a gap in the brick wall by a large hornbeam tree and across grass for 100 yards to a metalled track. Turn right for 100 yards to a marker post at the corner of alder windbreaks and through a gap into an apple orchard. The wayfinding becomes difficult here – the path goes diagonally slightly left through the orchard, ending about 12 trees from the right hand end at its far end. Here there is a gap in another windbreak and the path continues on a slightly left diagonal through another orchard and through another gap at a marker post. Go sharp right in front of some tall sweet chestnut trees to keep the windbreak on your right, following it as it bends left, then 150 yards on go right through a gap in it at a low stile and straight ahead on a wide track through a plum orchard. Enter trees, then continue between wire fences with a vineyard on the right and keep straight on, soon with an ivy-clad wall on the right, to a minor road.

A member of the lily family, the bog asphodel has lovely yellow, star-shaped flowers with orange stamens. The flowers are arranged in short spikes on leafless stems and provide a welcome splash of colour in July and August in boggy areas. As Kent has few bogs, this flower is rare in the county, but commoner in the wetter western and northern parts of Britain.

*D*ragonflies make an impressive sight as they zoom around near ponds and streams, spotting potential insect prey with their enormous eyes and catching it on the wing. The beautiful gauzy wings, with their intricate network of veins, can propel them around at speeds of up to 20 mph. The eggs are laid on aquatic plants and the nymphs, which are also ferocious predators, may live underwater for several years before emerging to moult into adults.

5 Turn left along the road for ³/₄ mile then left on a lane signposted to Hothfield. There is coniferous woodland on the left but the roadside fringe has deciduous trees such as hornbeam and field maple and there is honeysuckle in places. On the other verge are flowers such as agrimony, knapweeds, hedge bedstraw and meadow vetchling. After bends pass a house called High Ridge on the right and 300 yards on, as the lane veers right, go left up a trackway at a byway sign.

6 The sunken track goes between hedges of blackthorn, elder, field maple and hazel and can be muddy in places. Later it passes a bluebell wood, then crosses a stream and continues between fields. Flowers such as knapweeds and fleabane attract meadow brown and Essex skipper butterflies. At a road go straight across, through a gateway, and diagonally right across a large field, with views ahead to the North Downs. Along the path are arable weeds such as field pansy, hedge mustard, scentless mayweed and scarlet pimpernel. Cross a stile in a hedge and go straight on to enter a wood at another. Turn sharp left on a wide track and after 100 yards go right on a concrete path that soon crosses a bog with rushes, water mint and bird's-foot trefoil. It is important to keep to the paths as the boggy areas can be dangerous. When the concrete ends keep straight on to reach the marker post at Point 2. Retrace your steps from here by going right through the clump of birch trees, left on the grassy track and on the path through trees back to the road and car park.

PLACE OF INTEREST NEARBY
Godinton House and Garden, 2 miles south-east of Hothfield, has lovely gardens and trees surrounding a Jacobean house. Telephone: 01233 620773.

OARE MARSHES AND THE SWALE ESTUARY

– estuary and marsh

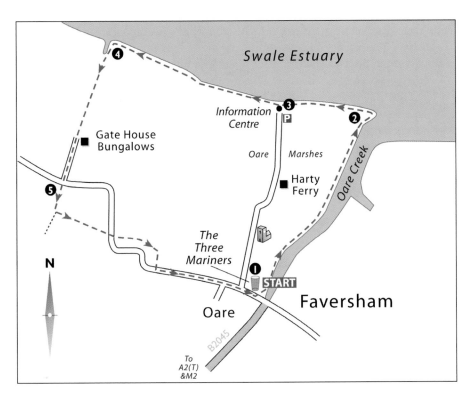

*T*his is a walk by river estuary and marshes, rich in birdlife. Huge flocks of waders and wildfowl can be seen on the river mudflats, marshes and lagoons, particularly in winter. These include beautiful and rare birds such as avocets and little egrets. Birds of prey such as owls and harriers hunt over the marshes, and on a smaller scale there are colourful dragonflies hunting for their insect prey over the drainage ditches. You may also be lucky enough to spot seals basking on sandbanks exposed in the estuary, so take your binoculars. There are also pleasant views of the yachts on the river estuary and across to the Isle of Sheppey.

THE WALK

1 From the front of the pub turn left for a few yards to the T-junction, then left again down the main street of the village. Just past another pub, the Castle, go left through a kissing gate at a Saxon Shore Way fingerpost. Go diagonally right across a field and through bushes to another kissing gate at the side of a creek with lots of sailing boats. Continue along the side of the creek, with saltmarsh plants such as golden samphire and sea lavender adding colour. On the left are marshes with drainage ditches, in which you may see swans, herons, or even a kingfisher. The creek widens out, with extensive mudflats on which gulls and oystercatchers probe for food, and the lilac flowers of sea aster can be seen on the creekside.

2 Keep on the creekside path as it swings left under power lines, then enters the Kent Wildlife Trust nature reserve of Oare Marshes. Keep straight on over a metal footbridge and past a flooded area on the

STARTING POINT: From the Three Mariners pub in Oare village, or alternatively from the car park at Oare Marshes nature reserve.

HOW TO GET THERE: From junction 6 of the M2 go north to the A2 then west. Just west of Faversham turn right off the A2 on the B2045 to reach Oare after 1^1/$_2$ miles. Turn left into the village and the Three Mariners is a few hundred yards along on the right. If continuing to the parking area at the nature reserve, turn right immediately after the pub to Harty Ferry. Oare is served by Arriva buses from Maidstone, Sittingbourne and Faversham.

PARKING: In the car park at the Three Mariners (with the landlord's permission) or at the car park at the information centre at Oare Marshes nature reserve (walk joined at Point 3).

REFRESHMENTS: The Three Mariners has a good selection of food and beers in comfortable surroundings. Telephone: 01303 260406.

LENGTH OF WALK: 4^1/$_2$ miles. Map: OS Explorer 149 Sittingbourne & Faversham (GR of pub 006629; of nature reserve car park 013648).

left, which often teems with birds such as teal, wigeon, coot, pintail duck, little grebe, shoveler, and even the striking little egret. The dykes and ditches are full of reeds, in which reed bunting, reed and sedge warblers and the rare bearded tit breed. The grazing marshes here are also vital for other birds such as redshank and lapwing, and recently the rare avocet, with its beautiful black and white plumage, has begun to breed here. Looking out over the estuary of the Swale, across to the Isle of Sheppey, you may be lucky enough to see seals basking on the sand banks that are exposed at low tide. On the mudflats are gulls, oystercatchers and waders such as curlew, knot, dunlin and greenshank.

3 Continue past the information centre (open at weekends) and car park at the Watch House, formerly a customs outpost. You can take a short-cut back to Oare village by going left along the road here, but otherwise continue along the path on the embankment alongside the estuary. Bird's-foot trefoil and sowthistles provide yellow splashes of colour, while thistles attract immigrant butterflies such as painted lady, red admiral and clouded yellow and grasshoppers chirrup in the long grass. In winter you may see short-eared owls or marsh harriers gliding over the marshes as they search for prey.

4 When the path swings inland by a creek with a few remains of a disused jetty continue inland on a path past a lagoon and through a metal gate, then on a wide grassy track with ditches on both sides. Dragonflies abound here in late summer, including the red sympetrum with its bright red body. Cross a stile and go through a gate between buildings, then straight along a gravel road, later passing a small cherry orchard.

5 On reaching a T-junction with a minor road you can turn left to follow the road back to Oare. However, to avoid some road walking, go straight

The striking, exotic-looking little egret was, until recently, a very rare visitor to Britain. However, a pair nested for the first time in Poole Harbour, Dorset in 1996 and recently the birds began to raise young at a few places in Kent. It is still a lovely surprise to spot the egret's snowy-white plumage, standing out against the background as it fishes in marshland lagoons or river estuaries.

A *few of the lovely clouded yellow butterflies reach the shores of Kent in most years, having travelled from southern Europe or even North Africa. Occasionally much larger numbers appear and they spread inland, stopping to feed on flowers, and sometimes breeding here to produce more butterflies later in the year. They are unable to survive the winter in Britain, so we rely on immigration.*

across the road, through a metal gate, and along the left edge of a field. Cross a stile, then go straight ahead on a path between a fence and a hedge laden with blackberries in autumn. At a cross-track turn left on it, with white flowers of yarrow at the sides. Where the track swings left go straight on over a stile then diagonally right across a field to a stile by a telegraph pole. Continue in the same direction across the next field, under power lines, to a road. Go right for 50 yards then left at a footpath sign to go diagonally right across a field, following a line of telegraph poles. There is soon an alder windbreak on the right and fine views across to the estuary looking left and back. Just after the last telegraph pole turn right along the right edge of a field to a road, then left to return to the village.

PLACE OF INTEREST NEARBY
Brogdale World of Fruit, 3 miles south of Oare, is home to the National Fruit Collection, with over 4,000 varieties of fruit trees and plants in 150 acres of rural Kent, plus tearoom, gift shop and plant sales centre. Follow signs from A2 at Faversham. Telephone: 01795 535286.

WYE DOWNS AND THE DEVIL'S KNEADING TROUGH

– *downland flowers and butterflies*

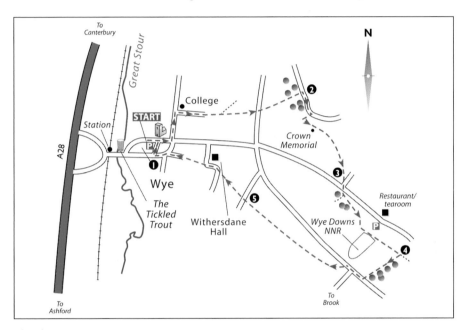

*T*he *beautiful countryside around the historic village of Wye is the setting for this walk, which takes you to a national nature reserve that has over 400 different wild flowers and 28 butterfly species, some of the highest numbers to be found anywhere in the country. The short downland turf can have as many as 40 different flowers per square metre. There is also a tremendous view over the Devil's Kneading Trough, a steep-sided valley formed by meltwater at the end of the last Ice Age. Because the walk goes through undulating countryside, it involves some fairly steep climbs and descents.*

THE WALK

1 Going out of the entrance to the car park opposite the green turn right past the church and the original buildings of Wye College,

67

then turn left into Olantigh Road. After 180 yards go right up Occupation Road, with the new Kempe building of the University on your left, and later glasshouses and field plots used for experiments. Keep straight on where the road becomes a wide stony track, with tall poplars then a hedge on the right. On reaching a minor road go straight across and gradually uphill, with a view on the right of a crown carved into the chalk, to enter a wood near a bush of wild privet, the flowers of which attract meadow brown, gatekeeper and ringlet butterflies in high summer. Keep to the main path through the wood to reach another minor road.

2 Turn right here, though it is worth a look in the field opposite, which is being managed under the Countryside Management scheme to enable chalkland flowers to flourish once again. Walk along the road, with herb robert, herb bennet, hedge woundwort and enchanter's nightshade on the banks and where the trees on the right end go right up steps at a North Downs Way (NDW) sign. Continue to a stile by a gate and on to another

STARTING POINT: At the public car park in the centre of Wye.

HOW TO GET THERE: Wye is reached on minor roads running east from the A28 between Ashford and Canterbury. Just past the railway station and the Tickled Trout turn left into Churchfield Way, to reach the car park on the right after 400 yards. Wye

is served by trains and Stagecoach-East Kent buses between Ashford and Canterbury.

PARKING: In the public car park off Churchfield Way in the centre of Wye.

REFRESHMENTS: There is a selection of pubs and restaurants in Wye. The Tickled Trout pub, just across the river from the station, is 400 yards from the start, is in a lovely setting and has a pleasant garden alongside the water. It serves good food and ales in very comfortable surroundings. Telephone: 01233 812227. Halfway round the route at Point 3 is the Devil's Kneading Trough Restaurant and Tearooms. They serve morning coffee, lunches and afternoon teas, in addition to evening meals and Sunday lunches. Telephone: 01233 813212.

LENGTH OF WALK: 5 miles. Map: OS Explorer 137 Ashford (GR 053468).

stile, after which you turn sharp left along the top of the slope with a wire fence on the left. The field on the right has many chalkland flowers, including the creamy white dropwort, yellow bird's-foot trefoil, lady's bedstraw and horseshoe vetch, blue milkwort and lilac scabious, and green woodpeckers can often be seen prospecting for ants. You soon pass the crown, with seats from which you can admire the fine views over the Stour Valley. Keep to the right of a wooden bench and along the top of the ridge to a kissing gate and continue with a wire fence on the left, then through a metal gate to a narrow road.

3 Turn right for 20 yards to a wider road and cross to enter a wood by an information board for the Wye Downs National Nature Reserve. After a few yards take the left fork (NDW) and go through trees to a marker post where they end. If you need refreshment you can go left here to the Devil's Kneading Trough Restaurant and Tearooms but the walk goes diagonally right to a gate then straight on with a fence on the right to reach the spectacular deep valley known as the Devil's Kneading Trough, carved out after the last Ice Age by meltwater cascading down the steep slope. It is well worth a diversion into the valley through the gate on the right, as this is one of the richest areas for flowers and butterflies in the county. The butterflies include three types of blue – common, chalkhill and the rare adonis blue. There are 19 different orchids here, including bee, fragrant and pyramidal, plus other colourful flowers such as yellow rock rose, blue and mauve milkwort and white and yellow eyebright. In addition, you may hear nightingales singing in the scrub, or spot fallow deer. After exploring, return to the gate and from the direction you were walking in

The colourful, exotic-looking flowers of the bee orchid have evolved to resemble a bee that is attracted to the flower in other parts of Europe and pollinates it. It can sometimes occur in quite large numbers on chalky soils, but its appearance is sporadic from year to year. Each flower can produce thousands of tiny seeds that are dispersed by the wind, but few of them will germinate successfully.

previously go diagonally left to a marker post then right along the top of the slope to a stile with NDW sign. Continue straight on for 400 yards then leave the NDW by going right at a wooden five-bar gate near bushes (there is an English Nature footpath sign behind the gate).

The males of the chalkhill blue butterfly are a lovely milky or silvery blue, while the females are brown. It is only found on certain areas on the chalk downs, where the food-plant of its caterpillars, horse-shoe vetch, grows. In these places it is sometimes possible to see large numbers in July, feeding on knapweeds and other flowers.

4 Go down the sunken path with a tall hedge on the left, then under coppiced hazel bushes. Further downhill the path opens out and there are common spotted and fragrant orchids on the banks at the side in June. The path emerges onto a minor road. Turn right to a junction and take the right fork, with wild hops in the hedge on the right. After 200 yards go left at a stile in the hedge and diagonally right across a field, then cross a farm track and continue to the right of a hedge. After crossing another track keep in the same direction, but to the left of a hedge. Continue along the right edge of fields and past an example of a layered hedge on the right to a minor road.

5 Go straight across the road and continue on a track that passes a cultivated hop garden, sheltered behind a tall beech hedge, then on a lane past the gardens of Withersdane Hall with walnut and lime trees. Where the lane bends right go straight on along a path past a sports field then a road between houses. On reaching a road on a bend keep straight on then take Church Road on the right to return to the church and car park.

PLACES OF INTEREST NEARBY

The **Agricultural Museum** at Brook, 3 miles south-east of Wye, has a fascinating collection of old agricultural implements and tools, including butter-making equipment, housed in a magnificent 14th century barn. Limited opening hours. Telephone: 01304 824969. **Canterbury's** many attractions, including the cathedral, are less than 10 miles from Wye.

WALK 15

APPLEDORE, THE ROYAL MILITARY CANAL AND WAREHORNE

– water-loving plants and birds

Starting at the historic village of Appledore this pleasant walk goes through the tranquil landscapes of Romney Marsh, with the evocative calls of lapwings and curlew. The first section is alongside the historic Royal Military Canal, home to swans, herons and other water birds and plants such as yellow water-lilies. The numerous drainage ditches in the area contain lovely flowers like water violet and purple loosestrife, while colourful dragonflies and damselflies fly over the water. You may hear the croaking of marsh frogs and see butterflies such as the rare white-letter hairstreak. This is one of the longer walks, but it is mainly flat. If you want a shorter circuit you can head westwards at Point 2, omitting the village of Warehorne and Kenardington church.

STARTING POINT: The village hall car park in Appledore.

HOW TO GET THERE: Appledore is on the B2080, which can be taken east from Tenterden or west from the A2070 at Brenzett. The car park is behind the village hall, on the west side of the main street through the village. Appledore is served by Stagecoach-East Kent buses. The railway station is 1¹⁄₄ miles east of the village.

PARKING: In the car park at Appledore village hall.

REFRESHMENTS: There are two pubs and a tearoom in the village. The Black Lion, near the church, serves a fine selection of food, including local lamb and fish from Hastings, plus real ales. Telephone: 01233 758206.

LENGTH OF WALK: 4¹⁄₂ or 7 miles. Map: OS Explorer 125 Romney Marsh (GR 956296).

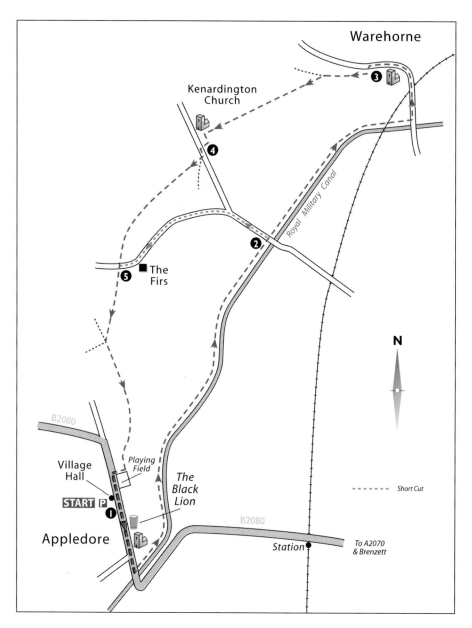

THE WALK

1 Going out of the car park, turn right down the main street of the village, with house martins swooping overhead in summer. Continue past the Black Lion and the church and go straight on with care down the road ahead (no footpath) where another road goes off right. After 150 yards, shortly before a bridge, go left at a Royal Military Canal Path fingerpost to the bank of the canal. Walk along the bank, or on the alternative path below it. This has a dyke to its left which has a variety of aquatic plants along its length, including the lovely lilac-coloured water violet in May, while later in the year there is the white of water crowfoot and water plantain, yellow loosestrife and bird's-foot trefoil and purple loosestrife. In summer the main canal is covered with yellow water lilies and you may see swans, herons, or even catch a glimpse of a kingfisher. Trees and shrubs include lovely silvery-green willows, ash, hawthorn, occasional holly and oak, and alders with their characteristic seed cones. Green-veined white butterflies and many types of dragonflies and damselflies fly over the aquatic vegetation, and there are reed and sedge warblers and water voles amongst it.

2 On reaching a narrow road after 2 miles, turn left on it if you want to do the shorter walk and avoid many of the stiles, keeping left where it forks to reach Point 5, where you go left at a stile shortly after passing a white house on the left called The Firs. Otherwise, for the longer walk go straight across the road and continue alongside the canal. In spring you may hear the booming noise of marsh frogs, introduced from eastern Europe in the 1930s, which have spread to most of the Romney Marsh area. The rather eerie cries of lapwings can also be heard in this area. After 3/4 mile the canal and path bend right and pass under a white-painted railway bridge. In this stretch a few elms have just about survived the ravages of Dutch elm disease and in July you may be

Purple loosestrife has the traditional name of 'long purples' because of its tall spikes of magenta flowers. These make a striking display alongside rivers and streams and in marshy areas from June to September and often attract white butterflies. Although never very common in Britain, it has become a serious weed in North America.

73

The pretty little white-letter hairstreak butterfly has become very rare in Kent since Dutch elm disease killed many of the elm trees on which its caterpillars feed. It now hangs on in a few places where elm grows as suckers or a few trees survive. It gets its name from the W-shape of the white line on the underside of the wing. The butterflies spend most of the time flying or sitting on leaves up in the canopy, but sometimes come down to feed on flowers.

lucky enough to see a white-letter hairstreak butterfly. These have become rare because their caterpillars depend on elm for food. At a minor road, shortly past the bridge, turn left and follow it to the village of Warehorne, then past the church and another excellent pub, the Woolpack.

3 About 250 yards past the pub go left along a farm road, but after 20 yards go right through a metal gate (no footpath sign). You are now following the Saxon Shore Way long distance footpath back to Appledore. Go straight across the field to a stile 50 yards to the right of a metal gate, then down the centre of a long field, with fine views to the left, to a stile hidden in the hedge. Aim towards a church in the distance as you continue diagonally left across a field to a post at the left end of a hedge at the far side. From the post keep in the same direction to the left of willows to reach a footbridge that crosses two dykes. Here there are brambles that attract meadow brown and gatekeeper butterflies and in the ditches are aquatic plants such as water plantain, water forget-me-not and rushes. Continue towards the church over several stiles and along the left edge of a field to enter the churchyard. At the church entrance porch go diagonally left to a stile by an oak tree, then right to follow the field boundary by a garden hedge to a minor road.

4 Go left for 10 yards then right over a stile. The path continues straight ahead across a large field (not diagonally left as the sign suggests), going towards the hedge on the left then parallel to it at a distance of 20 yards, before veering diagonally right near a telegraph pole. At a marker post by trees at the corner of a paddock, keep straight on along the left edge of a field to a stile by large oak and ash trees, then over a succession of stiles and steps and straight across a long field to reach a minor road.

5 Go straight across to a stile, then diagonally right across a field to a plank bridge by a large ash tree and straight across the next field to a gap in a hedge. Continue straight across the next field, just to the left of the first telegraph pole, to a marker post to the left of a line of trees. As the path climbs gradually there are far-reaching views over Romney Marsh to Dungeness power station and back to the North Downs in the far distance. Bear right at the post, past the line of oak trees on the right to another post where they end. Go diagonally left here, over a mound topped with trees, and down a field under power lines to a stile near two large oak trees. Continue straight on across a small field to a plank bridge hidden in the hedge in the far corner, then diagonally left across the next field towards houses. At a post at the far side turn left past back gardens then right through a metal gate and along a tarmac track to a road. Turn left for 300 yards to return to the car park.

PLACE OF INTEREST NEARBY
South of England Rare Breeds Centre has friendly farm animals, a large playground, woodland walks, a restaurant and a picnic area. At Woodchurch, 3 miles north of Appledore. Telephone: 01233 861493.

BLEAN WOODS
– *nightingales and fritillaries*

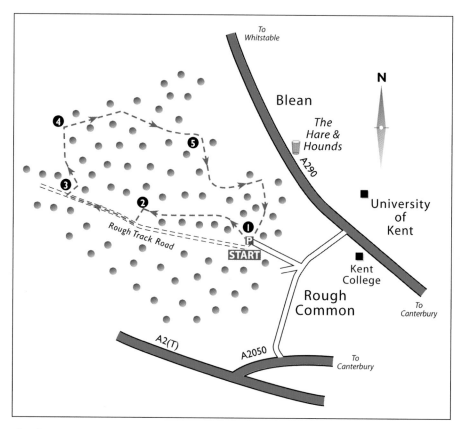

*T*his area of ancient broad-leaved woodland is extremely important for wildlife, especially birds and butterflies, and fortunately it is now preserved and under the care of various conservation organisations. As you walk through the woods, you can admire some fine trees and you may hear the tuneful singing of a nightingale, as this is one of their strongholds in Britain. There are also colourful wild flowers, particularly evident in spring, and you may see the rare heath fritillary butterfly in summer. This walk is mostly flat and without stiles. There are also shorter walks available from the car park, waymarked by the RSPB.

THE WALK

1 From the large notice board in the RSPB car park take a path at a wooden post with arrows in several colours. Most of the walk follows the route marked by black arrows, but takes a shorter route at one stage. The path goes through groves of silver birch and sweet chestnut, with heather and gorse in places. Continue straight across a cross-track, then take the left fork at the next marker post. You soon come to a clearing where birds such as linnets, whitethroats and tree pipits breed and where there are mauve devil's-bit scabious and yellow fleabane and goldenrod flowers in late summer. Keep straight on at the next cross-track to reach an area of heathland, purple with heather. This is an important area for rare nightjars, whose distinctive churring sound may be heard, usually at dusk. You will also start to see the large mound-shaped nests of wood ants, made with pine needles and other plant material. Trails of these large ants lead to and from the nest, carrying plant material and items of insect prey. Go left at the next

STARTING POINT: At the RSPB nature reserve car park at Rough Common.

HOW TO GET THERE: Rough Common is 2 miles north-west of Canterbury. Take the A290 from Canterbury to Whitstable and turn left to Rough Common. Alternatively, from the A2(T) take the A2050 and turn off left to Rough Common. The RSPB reserve is signposted from the village. Stagecoach-East Kent buses run from Canterbury to Rough Common and, more frequently, along the A290 about ¹/₂ mile from the start.

PARKING: In the car park at the RSPB's Blean Woods nature reserve at Rough Common.

REFRESHMENTS: At Blean, on the A290, ¹/₂ mile north of the turning to Rough Common, is the Hare & Hounds, which incorporates Angelo's Restaurant and serves breakfast, morning coffee, lunches and bar meals as well as evening dinners, all in pleasant surroundings. Telephone: 01227 471594. There is also a pub in Rough Common and many pubs, tearooms and restaurants in Canterbury, only 2 miles from the start.

LENGTH OF WALK: 4 miles. Map: OS Explorer 150 Canterbury & the Isle of Thanet (GR 122594).

fork through an area of large oak trees and straight across at the next cross-track to go through more oak woodland with ferns beneath. This oak woodland supports a great variety of birds, including woodpeckers, tits, nuthatches and tree creepers.

2 At the next wide cross-track go left, still following the black arrows. These wide tracks or 'rides' through the woods are kept open, as they form an important habitat for butterflies and flowers. You will see meadow brown, gatekeeper, comma and speckled wood butterflies here and flowers such as bright pink betony. After about 400 yards you reach a wide, stony cross-track, just before a small Woodland Trust sign. Turn right along this track, leaving the 'black walk' for a while. Alongside the track are flowers such as yellow tormentil and fleabane and purple rosebay willowherb.

3 After ½ mile look for another stony track going off on the right and soon curving right (just past the track is a post with a black arrow on the opposite side). Turn right on this track, to now follow the black arrows again for the remainder of the walk. After 400 yards turn left at a marker post to a T-junction of paths after 30 yards and turn left again. Notice a gnarled old oak trunk here: this tree is over 500 years old and the shape is the result of pollarding, ie cutting back its branches at regular intervals. You go through more oak and sweet chestnut woodland, where the lovely song of the nightingale may be heard in May and June. After a while fields are visible on the left and the path goes under hornbeams, identifiable by their bunches of winged seeds, a favourite food of hawfinches.

The lovely heath fritillary butterfly is now very rare in Britain, being confined to Kent, Essex and south-west England. It almost became extinct in Kent in the 1980s, but in the nick of time research indicated the management that was needed to save it. The woods north of Canterbury where it still occurs are now managed by conservation organisations, who coppice the trees to allow the foodplant of the caterpillars, cow-wheat, to grow better. This has resulted in a large increase in numbers and the bright orange and black adults may be seen feeding on the flowers of bramble in June and July.

4 As the wood ends turn right at a T-junction of paths near an English Nature information board by a

The comma butterfly can be recognised by the ragged outline to the lovely orange and black wings. The undersides of the wings are dark brown, making it difficult to see when at rest, and have the pale comma-shaped mark that gives it the name. The caterpillars feed on hop leaves, of which there are plenty in the hedgerows of Kent, and on nettles. Adult butterflies are often seen feeding on ivy flowers and ripe fruit in autumn.

large oak tree. The path soon becomes a wide shale track through dense hornbeam coppice. Keep straight on at the first marker post then right at a pair of posts. Notice the luxuriant mosses on the ground beneath the trees here and you may see poisonous fly agaric toadstools, red with white spots. You reach a more open area where you keep straight on. This area is kept clear of trees to encourage the growth of cow-wheat, which is the foodplant of the caterpillars of the rare heath fritillary butterfly. You may see this lovely orange and black butterfly in June and early July. Continue straight on at the marker post at the end of the open area.

5 At the next marker post by another English Nature notice board go right to another post after 10 yards, then straight on. After 300 yards go left and keep on this path as it later curves right by a post with black and red arrows. In places there are colourful flowers in spring, before the leaves of the trees create shade, including bluebells, violets, wood anemones and yellow archangel. Later in the year there are fragrant patches of lily-of-the-valley beneath the old beech trees. Follow the black arrow markers straight on for a while then to the right to return to the car park.

PLACES OF INTEREST NEARBY
The **Roman Museum** in the centre of Canterbury has the remains of a Roman house with a fine mosaic floor and exquisite silver and glass. Telephone: 01227 785575. **Wildwood** is a wildlife discovery park set in woodland, with a fine selection of British animals, including otters, badgers and wolves, plus an adventure playground. On the A291 between Canterbury and Herne Bay. Telephone: 01227 712111.

GROVE FERRY AND STODMARSH
– reedbeds and riverbank

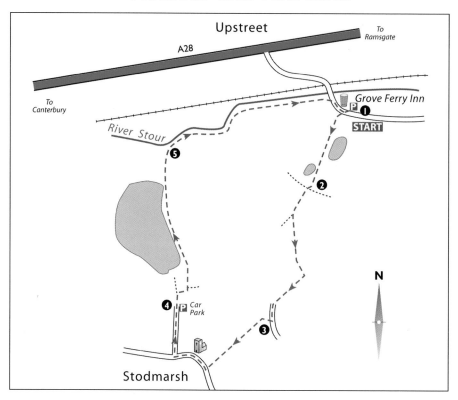

*A*n atmospheric walk as the wind whispers through the reedbeds of Stodmarsh National Nature Reserve. Most of the walk is within the reserve, and the hides there provide opportunities to view many rare and common birds, including kingfishers and bearded tits. This is also one of the few areas in Britain where the elusive bittern occurs and if you are extremely lucky you may hear the characteristic booming call of the male. There are also open areas of water that attract large numbers of wildfowl and wading birds. At the end of the walk there is a lovely stretch alongside the River Stour, with its swans, mallards and other water birds and riverside plants. A flat walk, but parts of it can be quite wet underfoot after heavy rain, when waterproof footwear is advisable.

THE WALK

1 From the entrance to the car park cross the road and go down a ramp with wooden hand rails and right on a path that runs parallel to the road. After 50 yards turn left on another gravel track by an information board. Yellow lichens grow on the bark of dead elms in the scrub on the right. A little way on it is worth taking a short diversion off the main path to a raised viewing platform on the left. This overlooks a lake, where you may see birds such as greylag and white-fronted geese, cormorants, lapwings, shoveler duck, redshank and moorhens. Back on the grassy path continue between extensive reedbeds, home to reed and sedge warblers, reed buntings and the rare water rail. Off to the right is another hide, from which kingfishers and bearded tits may be seen. Continue past open water on the right, in which the ferny-looking milfoil grows, then the path bends left to reach a T-junction with a wide stony track.

2 Go right on the track for 15 yards then left through a metal kissing gate on a path alongside a dyke on the left, then veering away from it

STARTING POINT: At the public car park at Grove Ferry picnic site. An alternative starting point is the car park at the Stodmarsh end of the nature reserve (Point 4), from where there are shorter marked nature trails, including one suitable for wheelchairs.

HOW TO GET THERE: From the A28 between Canterbury and Margate turn off south at Upstreet to reach the picnic site after ¼ mile. Stagecoach-East Kent buses serve Upstreet.

PARKING: In the car park at Grove Ferry picnic site.

REFRESHMENTS: The Grove Ferry Inn is adjacent to the picnic site and serves fine meals. It has a large garden, with a children's playground at the end, and in summer you can take a boat trip from here along the river. Notice also the impressive horse chestnut trees in front of the inn. Telephone: 01227 860302.

LENGTH OF WALK: 4 miles. Map: OS Explorer 150 Canterbury & the Isle of Thanet (GR of Grove Ferry picnic site 236631; of car park at Stodmarsh reserve GR 222609).

to a footbridge. Cross this, then after 30 yards go left over another footbridge, then diagonally right across a field to a stile by a metal gate. Go left on a farm track for 20 yards then right over a stile and diagonally left across a field to two footbridges over ditches, the second 30 yards diagonally left of the first. These ditches and dykes are essential for drainage and provide homes for water voles, frogs and toads and plants such as frogbit, great water dock, and the pink amphibious bistort. Continue diagonally left across a field to a metal gate, then turn right on a grassy track, with lots of dragonflies zooming over the ditch on the right. Go through another gate and past tall poplars and a farm on the left to a stony track and keep straight on along it between hedges festooned with ivy and bramble.

3 As the track bends left go over a stile in a gap on the right (footpath 136) and slightly diagonally right across a small field to another stile.

Continue straight ahead, soon on a wide gravel track. You may see the attractive orange and black wall brown butterfly here, now rather uncommon, and the pink flowers of mallow. The track becomes a tarmac road as it passes a farm and continues to a minor road near a thatched cottage. Turn right along the road to reach the hamlet of Stodmarsh. The road bends left by the tiny church, then 30 yards on turn right up a lane, though you may first wish to visit another excellent pub, the Red Lion, just past the lane. The lane has hedges of hawthorn and elder, with climbers such as bramble, wild rose, hops and ivy clambering over it. The ivy flowers attract many wasps, flies and late red admiral and comma butterflies in autumn. At the end of the lane is a car park for Stodmarsh National Nature Reserve.

The lapwing gets its name from its flapping, broad-winged flight and its alternative name of pee-wit from the sound of its calls, rather eerie when heard through a mist on the marshes. They can occur in large flocks but numbers have declined in recent years as a result of changes in farming practices. Feeding on the ground on worms and insect grubs, they can be recognised by the wispy black crest on the head. The plumage looks white and black at a distance, but close-up the dark areas are a lovely green.

4 Continue on the track going to the left of the car park, past a gate saying 'English Nature', and on a track lined by hazel bushes. Where the

The lovely pink flowers of the common mallow often brighten up roadsides, hedges and waste places. The plants can become rather tall and straggly, but the individual flowers are very beautiful when viewed close up, with their darker pink veining. The Romans used to eat the flowers, leaves and seeds.

track forks by information board no 6 go right, though there is the option to visit another hide by going straight on then returning. At the next fork keep left to go straight on with a ditch and reedbeds on the left and tall alders on the right. Soon there is a lake on the left and you pass a tower hide overlooking it. If you are really lucky you may catch a glimpse of the rare and secretive bittern, which now breeds here, though you are more likely to see its commoner relative, the grey heron. Sand martins can often be seen flying over the lakes to catch insects. Alongside the track the flat white flowerheads of hogweed attract hoverflies and soldier beetles, while the teasel flowers are popular with peacock butterflies and later goldfinches take the seeds. The raised bank on which the path runs is known as the Lampen Wall and was built by Flemish engineers in the early 18th century to prevent flooding.

5 The path bends right to follow the bank of the Great Stour river, with lots of willows and sallows, whose yellow, nectar-rich catkins provide food for bumble bees and butterflies in spring. You are likely to see swans and mallard ducks on the river, while over the grazing marshes on the right birds of prey hunt for food. You may see a kestrel hovering, or glimpse a rarer predator such as a marsh or hen harrier or short-eared owl. On the river banks are purple flowers of comfrey and white yarrow. Continue on the path until a road is reached, then cross it to the left to the pub and car parks beyond.

PLACE OF INTEREST NEARBY
Wingham Wildlife Park has a wide variety of animals and birds, including monkeys, wallabies and meerkats, plus an adventure playground. It is 3 miles south of Grove Ferry, on the A257. Telephone: 01227 722053.

THE ELHAM VALLEY

– *downland flowers and valley views*

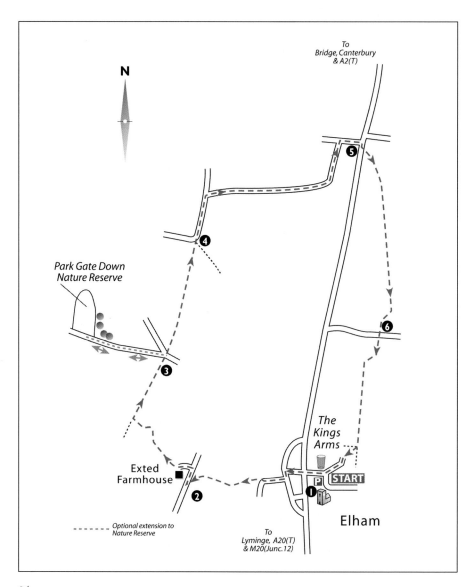

*T*his walk starts at the lovely village of Elham, which has several half-timbered buildings, and explores the delightful rolling countryside of the Elham Valley. There is a gradual climb up the side of the valley through a meadow colourful with cowslips and other flowers. Later there is an opportunity to visit a nature reserve renowned for its displays of wild orchids. The walk continues on field paths and quiet lanes, with lovely views, and returns to the village along the tree-lined Nailbourne stream, along the route of the defunct Elham Valley Railway. It is an undulating walk, with several gradual climbs and descents.

THE WALK

1 From the square in front of the church walk up to the main village street then go straight across and up the road to the left of the lovely black and white timbered building called 'Abbot's Fireside'. After a short distance turn left at a T-junction, then after 100 yards go right up Cullens Hill Lane. At the crest of the hill, where the lane bends left, keep straight on down a narrow path to the left of the garage of 'Quinces'. Cross a stile and descend a bank with flowers such as cowslips in spring and bird's-foot trefoil and red clover in summer, then cross a field to another stile. Continue across another field to a path between hedges and

STARTING POINT: In Elham village square, in front of the church.

HOW TO GET THERE: From junction 12 of the M20 go west on the A20(T) then north on a minor road through Lyminge. Once in Elham, take the second right into St Mary's Road, which leads to the village square. Stagecoach-East Kent buses between Canterbury and Folkestone stop at Elham.

PARKING: In Elham village square, near the church.

REFRESHMENTS: There are three pubs and a restaurant in the village. The Kings Arms, in the square, is a friendly inn which provides a fine range of food and drink. Telephone: 01303 840242.

LENGTH OF WALK: 5$^{1}/_{4}$ miles. Map: OS Explorer 138 Dover, Folkestone and Hythe (GR 177438).

keep in the same direction as it goes gradually uphill, shaded by blackthorn and field maple bushes and with hart's-tongue ferns on the hedgebanks. Keep to the main path as it bends left to reach a minor road opposite cottages.

2 Turn right along the road for 60 yards, then go left up a narrow lane. Immediately past Exted Farmhouse go left on a stony track that bends round between corrugated iron barns. Go through a metal gate into a field that has plenty of thistles to attract butterflies such as painted ladies and red admirals. Follow the track, with a wire fence on the left, then keep right of a short row of hornbeam trees to a metal gate and straight across a field with some poppies. Go through a gap in the hedge on to a track and turn right. Follow this track, with a hedge on the left containing oak, hawthorn, hazel, elder, wild rose and honeysuckle to eventually reach a road.

It is well worth a diversion here to the nearby Kent Wildlife Trust nature reserve at Park Gate Down (adds about $3/4$ mile). In spring there is a wonderful display of cowslips and early purple orchids, followed in early summer by a mass of other orchids, including fragrant, pyramidal and common spotted as well as other uncommon plants such as yellow rattle. Go sharp left along the narrow road for just over $1/4$ mile. Shortly after passing a small wood, with bluebells in spring, the reserve is on the right, with a gate by an information board. Contrast the wealth of wild flowers here with the impoverished flora of the agriculturally 'improved' grassland you walk through elsewhere on the walk. Retrace your footsteps down the lane to Point 3.

The lovely golden yellow flowers of cowslips, nodding in the breeze, are a much less familiar sight in spring than they used to be. However, they are making something of a comeback as their seed is sown alongside roads, and can still be found naturally on parts of the Downs. The name is said to derive from 'cow-slop', because they were believed to grow from cow pats.

The lovely fragrant orchid has long cylindrical spikes of densely-packed pink or lilac flowers in June and early July. Each flower has a long slender spur extending from the back and a fragrant scent, especially strong in the evening. The flower spikes can be as much as 18 inches (45 cm) tall. There can be large colonies in a few places on the chalk grassland of the Downs.

3 From your original direction go straight across the two narrow roads at the junction to a gate, rather hidden in trees, leading into a garden. Keep to the right edge of the garden to another gate, then go straight ahead through a field past tall oak and ash trees to a stile, continuing with a wire fence on the right and pleasant views over the valley. Where the fence ends continue through the centre of a meadow, then keep slightly left to pass a clump of trees on the right before going between a tall hornbeam tree on the left and a sunken area on the right. Keep close to the left edge of the next meadow, just below a line of trees, and past a small pond in the far corner to a stile. Continue along the left edge of the next field with a hedge on the left of field maple, holly and hazel, entwined with honeysuckle in places, to reach a metal gate to a road.

4 Turn right along the lane, with white hedge bedstraw on the right and later wild roses. Soon turn right down another lane under overhanging bushes, with pink herb robert and red campion and delicate quaking grass growing on the shady banks. As the lane opens out look out for patches of colourful yellow meadow vetchling on the banks and you may see a yellowhammer perched on a hedge. At the bottom of the hill the lane swings left to a T-junction. Turn right to a main road.

5 Cross with extreme care on the corner, going right for 80 yards then left at a stile down a concrete track. You are now following the Elham Valley Way long-distance footpath. Go diagonally left up the field, aiming for a stile next to a gate in a gap in a line of trees. Continue with a hedge and fence on the right. Follow a line of posts with yellow arrows to a stile, with a view to Elham village ahead, then between a hedge and a slope, before veering away from the hedge to the next marker post at the corner of a wire fence. Continue straight on, keeping to the right edge of a field, to a stile in the far right corner, then follow more posts through shorter turf, studded with blue milkwort and purple selfheal, to a stile. Take another stile to the right after 10 yards and go diagonally left across a field to a gate, then a road.

6 Go right for 30 yards then left up steps to a stile. Follow the path along the right edge of fields, shortly with tall poplars and a stream on the right, noticing the occasional purple-red flowers of hedge woundwort. Just before the village go through a metal gate on the right, over the stream and diagonally left across a small field to another gate, then up a narrow lane which ends at the village square.

PLACE OF INTEREST NEARBY
Elham Valley Vineyard has wines to sample, tours of the vineyards, pottery and craft shop. At Breach, 3 miles north of Elham. Telephone: 01227 831266.

SANDWICH BAY

– sea breezes and beaches

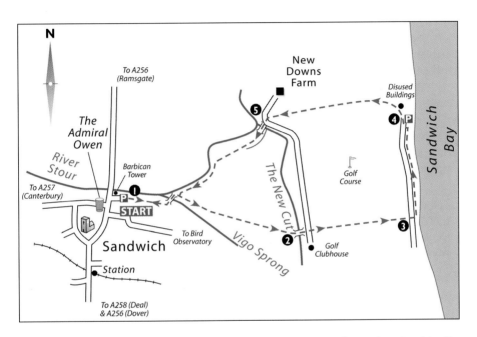

*S*tarting from the ancient and picturesque town of Sandwich, this flat walk provides the opportunity to get some sea air and to enjoy a variety of flowers, birds and butterflies. You can see colourful plants of the shingle beach, unusual orchids, and the many birds that feed at the tideline of the shore. The halfway point is at the beach, where you could search for marine life that has been washed up – or just sit and look out to sea! The final part of the walk goes alongside a river, its water and reedbeds home to swans, herons, warblers and other birds.

THE WALK

1 From the end of the car park away from the town and the Barbican Tower go past a gate and on a wide tarmac path between weeping willows and large plane trees, with the River Stour on the left. Shortly after passing a children's playground cross a branch of the river over a white

89

metal footbridge, looking out for herons, moorhens and other birds on the mud at the sides of the water. Continue diagonally right on a tarmac path, and where another path leaves on the left after 200 yards keep straight on. This is part of the Saxon Shore Way footpath and goes between poplars and hawthorns, then between fields and later blackthorn hedges.

2 On reaching another footbridge over water, cross it and go straight across a minor road and on to a kissing gate, with a golf clubhouse to the right. Cross a gravel track, then the path goes on a slight diagonal to the right. The next section across the golf course is marked by yellow-topped concrete posts at intervals – keep to the path and watch out for flying golf balls! The 'rough' of the golf course is very important for wildlife, with rare wild flowers, such as the strange-looking lizard orchids which grow here and hardly anywhere else in Britain. There are also commoner but beautiful flowers such as blue-mauve viper's bugloss, very popular with bees, yellow lady's bedstraw and stonecrop, pink storksbill

STARTING POINT: At the quayside by the ancient Barbican Tower in Sandwich. An important port in the past, the boats moored here now are pleasure cruisers and there are boat trips available. Grassy areas by the river make a pleasant place for a picnic.

HOW TO GET THERE: From the A258 turn off northwards to Sandwich. Go past the railway station and follow the one-way system round New Street, Harnet Street and right along Strand Street to a T-junction. Turn left towards Ramsgate but go immediately right before the Barbican Tower and bridge onto the quayside. Stagecoach-East Kent buses serve Sandwich, and the railway station is ½ mile from the start.

PARKING: In the large public car park on the quayside in Sandwich.

REFRESHMENTS: There are many pubs and restaurants in Sandwich, and the Little Cottage tearooms are on the quay. The Admiral Owen is one of the nearest pubs to the start. Dating from the 15th century, it has cosy bars and a good selection of ales and food. Telephone: 01304 620869.

LENGTH OF WALK: 4 miles. Map: OS Explorer 150 Canterbury & the Isle of Thanet (GR 333582).

and restharrow and white yarrow. The colourful common blue and small copper butterflies can be seen here too. The mown grass path eventually ends at a road in front of the shingle beach.

3 Turn left along the grassy area on the far side of the road. Here and on the shingle bank are plants adapted to seashore life such as sea holly and yellow horned-poppy, and there are broomrapes, which grow as parasites on the roots of the sea holly. The mauve flowers of the sea holly are often visited by butterflies such as painted ladies and red admirals that have flown in over the sea from continental Europe and need to replenish their energy reserves. It is also worth looking at the birds on the beach, where there may be several species of gulls, oystercatchers, shelduck, dunlin, redshank and ringed plovers. Continue for ¼ mile as far as some boarded-up houses and cross back to the road.

4 Just before the houses, with their resident house martins hunting for insects in summer, go diagonally left on a footpath at a marker post for the Stour Valley Walk to a stony path back across the golf course. A little way on is a wet area on the right with rushes, where rare marsh helleborines and purple-red southern marsh orchids flower in June and early July. There is also pink ragged robin and yellow fleabane, which attracts small heath butterflies. Where the track curves right, with pyramidal orchids in the grass on the right, go straight on across a mown grassy area, with a ditch on the left. At the far end, 50 yards to the right of the ditch, you will see a marker post by a gate. Continue from there to the next tall marker post, then keep on the well-worn path through rough grass, ignoring stiles on the right, to go to the left of a house and across a field to a stile at a minor road.

Viper's bugloss can provide a glorious splash of colour on sandy or chalky soils. Its blue-mauve flowers are popular with bumble bees, and their humming is audible around the plants. The name probably comes from the long red stamens that protrude from the flowers like the tongue of a snake, or from the fruits, which resemble the head of an adder or viper. It has become a serious weed in Australia and the USA.

5 Turn left along the road, but as it bends left after 10 yards go straight on along a stony track to soon cross a

The red admiral migrates to Britain from continental Europe annually, then breeds here on nettles to produce home-bred butterflies later in the year. These striking velvety black, red and white butterflies are often seen feeding on buddleia or ivy flowers, or becoming inebriated on the juices of ripe plums, pears or apples. Some adults have managed to survive the recent mild winters in Kent – the first time this has happened.

branch of the river, often with elegant swans on the water. Continue with the main river on the right, full of rushes which hide reed and sedge warblers, and later with lilac sea aster and golden samphire, flowering between July and October. On reaching a T-junction of paths turn right for a few yards to retrace your steps to the footbridge over the river, then right to the car park and town.

PLACES OF INTEREST NEARBY

Richborough Roman Fort (English Heritage) once guarded the busy entrance port to the Roman province of Britain. The massive stone walls remain and the fascinating museum houses finds from the site. One mile north of Sandwich off the A256, or it can be reached by boat trip from Sandwich Quay. Telephone: 01304 612013. **Sandwich Bird Observatory** is a centre for bird watching and recording, 1 mile east of Sandwich. Telephone: 01304 617341.

WALK 20

ST MARGARET'S AND THE WHITE CLIFFS

– white cliffs and sea views

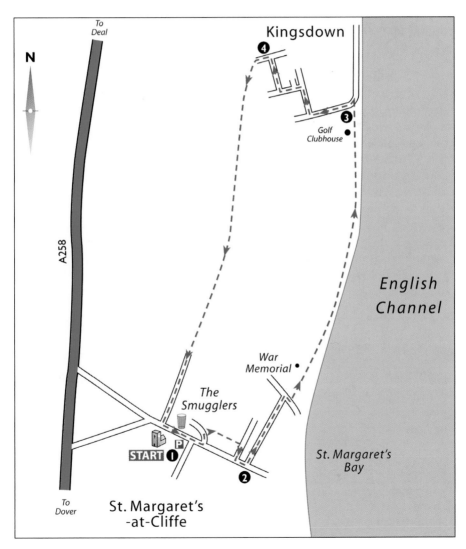

This stunning walk along the white cliffs of the Channel coast provides the opportunity to get some bracing sea air, whilst taking in some glorious views over the sea to France. You are accompanied by the cries of seabirds, while at your feet, in summer, are many colourful wild flowers which attract brightly coloured butterflies and day-flying burnet moths. From the cliffs the walk goes down to a beach before returning on an inland route, past scrub that provides a refuge for hundreds of birds on their migrations over the sea to and from Europe and Africa.

THE WALK

1 From the public car park walk to the main street through the village near to the Norman church, with the Smugglers pub opposite, and turn right. Go past the Hope Inn and turn left into Chapel Lane. Where the lane swings left go off right, down Droveway Gardens. Follow the concrete track as it bends right past houses, then between fields and houses, to a road. Turn right for 100 yards to another road then left for a short distance to a large grassy area with fine views to the sea.

STARTING POINT: At the car park near the church in St Margaret's-at-Cliffe.

HOW TO GET THERE: St Margaret's-at-Cliffe is reached by minor roads going east from the A258 to the north of Dover. The public car park is on the right just past the church. Stagecoach-East Kent buses serve St Margaret's.

PARKING: In the public car park near the church in St Margaret's-at-Cliffe.

REFRESHMENTS: There are four pubs in the village to choose from for refreshment. The Smugglers has a cosy bar and a dining area in a conservatory at the rear. There is also a sunny outdoor paved area. It serves a range of real ales and food, including Mexican specialities. Telephone: 01304 853404.

LENGTH OF WALK: 6 miles. Map: OS Explorer 138 Dover, Folkestone & Hythe (GR 358447).

2 Turn left here down Granville Road. On reaching a junction go down a minor road on the right, but after 30 yards go left through a gate. There are lovely views here back over St Margaret's Bay. Go straight on to a marker post. The next part of the walk follows the cliff path, with much of the land owned and managed by the National Trust. There is a wonderful variety of colourful wild flowers to be seen in summer – blue harebells and viper's bugloss, pink centaury and mallow, and yellow agrimony, bird's-foot trefoil and yellow-wort. There are also fragrant herbs such as thyme and marjoram and these and the purple knapweeds are particularly popular with the marbled white and meadow brown butterflies that abound here. Continue with the war memorial about 100 yards to your left unless you need refreshment, in which case you may want to visit the excellent Blue Bird tearooms in the old coastguard station on the left. As you continue along the clifftop path there are fine views over the English Channel to the French coast and you are accompanied by soaring gulls, swooping martins and the sound of skylarks. Orange-red soldier beetles mass on the heads of wild carrot and red and black burnet moths fly around flowers, including the vivid pink pyramidal orchids. An everlasting sweet pea, with bright purplish-crimson flowers, scrambles over the clifftop grass. After 1½ miles you pass a golf clubhouse on the left and go down steps to a road.

3 You could spend some time on the beach here – an ideal spot to refresh your feet in the sea on warm days. Otherwise turn sharp left along Oldstairs Road, with patches of hemp agrimony on the left attracting butterflies, then at a junction go sharp right to follow the road. Where overhanging trees end and before houses start, turn left along a narrow lane called Northcote Road, then after 200 yards turn right up Queensdown Road.

A lovely butterfly with a striking pattern of chequered black and white on the uppersides of the wings, the marbled white is quite numerous on some parts of the North Downs, including the tops of the white cliffs. It likes to visit flowers such as knapweeds and thistles to extract nectar using its long tongue. The caterpillars feed on various grasses.

4 At the top of this unmade road turn left and where the last garden on the right ends go diagonally left on a

*B*urnet moths are often mistaken for butterflies because they are brightly coloured and fly during the day. Their striking red and black coloration warns birds that they are dangerous to eat, as the body contains cyanide. This is why they can fly and feed in daylight with impunity. Their caterpillars feed on bird's-foot trefoil and you may see the papery cocoons containing the pupae attached to grass stems. The moth pictured is feeding on the nectar of a pyramidal orchid, and in the process will pollinate the orchid.

path across a field (not straight on along the track). The path continues to the right of a hedge with hawthorn, elder and bramble then past blackthorn thickets on the left before going between hedges. This scrubby vegetation provides a haven for a variety of small birds such as chiffchaffs, blackcaps and whitethroats, particularly during the main migration periods in spring and autumn. Keep straight on across a field to reach a tarmac track and turn right. More flowers can be seen alongside the track, including hogweed, hedge bedstraw and yarrow, all with white flowers, and patches of vivid purple tufted vetch. Continue on the track with a tall hedge on the left, often with gatekeeper butterflies flying around it, and the banks yellow with kidney vetch, bird's-foot trefoil and lady's bedstraw. After 1/2 mile the track reaches a road between houses. Follow this to the main street through the village, where you turn left to return to the car park.

PLACE OF INTEREST NEARBY
Dover Castle (English Heritage) has 2,000 years of history within its massive walls, including a Roman lighthouse, a medieval castle and secret World War II tunnels. Telephone: 01304 211067.